WORKING WITH GROUPS ON
SPIRITUAL
T H E M E S

D0972796

WORKING WITH GROUPS ON
SPIRITUAL
T H E M E S

STRUCTURED
EXERCISES
IN HEALING

VOLUME 2

ELAINE HOPKINS   ZO WOODS   RUSSELL KELLEY
KATRINA BENTLEY   JAMES MURPHY

WHOLE PERSON ASSOCIATES
Duluth, Minnesota

Library of Congress Cataloging in Publication Data 94-61707
ISBN 1-57025-048-0

REPRODUCTION POLICY

Unless otherwise noted, your purchase of this volume entitles you to reproduce a modest quantity of the worksheets that appear in this book for your education/ training activities. For this limited worksheet reproduction no special additional permission is needed. However the following statement, in total, must appear on all copies that you reproduce:

Reproduced from *Working with Groups on Spiritual Themes*
Copyright © 1995 by Sacred Heart Medical Center
Whole Person Associates, 210 W Michigan, Duluth, MN 55802.

Specific prior written permission is required from the publisher for any reproduction of a complete or adapted exercise with trainer instructions, or large-scale reproduction of worksheets, or for inclusion of material in another publication. Licensing or royalty arrangement requests for this usage must be submitted in writing and approved prior to any such use.

For further information please write for our Permissions Guidelines and Standard Permissions Form. Permission requests must be submitted at least 30 days in advance of your scheduled printing or reproduction.

Printed in the United States of America

10 9 8 7 6 5 4 3 2 1

WHOLE PERSON ASSOCIATES
210 W Michigan
Duluth MN 55802-1908
800-247-6789

ACKNOWLEDGMENTS

The authors gratefully acknowledge the support of the following people for their contributions to theme development: Candy Cooper, R.N., Cheryl Knott, R.N., C., Brenda Lenhart, M.Ed, Zonia Likkel, R.N., C., Laurie Lordan, R.N., C., Stephen Murphy, L.P.N., Toni Rowley, R.N., Val Spartz, R.N., C., Dean Tabish, R.N., C., Em Von Lanken, M.S., M.Ed, Paulette Wiedmer, R.N., and Jan Witt, R.N.

For their contributions to group development, we thank Gaea Aeolus, R.N., C., Pam Blume, R.N., C., Robin Cucilich, R.N., C., Sue Mauro, R.N., Terri Schmidt, L.P.N., and Jerry Woodke, R.N.

We would also like to thank Sue Baily, Sue Drury, and Tami Pogue, Health Unit Coordinators, for their many hours spent organizing materials, and Lorna Van Lankeren, Department of Psychiatry, for her hours spent at the word processor. A special thanks goes to all the staff of Main East, who have supported and facilitated the spirituality group.

We gratefully acknowledge Merrybeth Root and Scott Manning for allowing us to include the fine and fun poetry of the late Richard Reed Root and Dovie Lee Manning with our exercises.

FOREWORD

Spirituality is a key component within each person. Striving for wholeness is one of the dimensions deserving attention on life's continuum. For total health care, the physical, psychosocial, and spiritual dimensions comprise the totality of personhood and address the needs and concerns of persons from a holistic perspective.

Working with Groups on Spiritual Themes, developed by the nursing staff at the Sacred Heart Medical Center, Main East Psychiatric Unit in Spokane, Washington, is an excellent document for guiding group work in spiritual awareness with people in various settings. The material contained in this book will help group leaders initiate discussion on spiritual needs in a logical, organized fashion that should induce a high level of comfort for the group members and for the leaders.

Working with Groups on Spiritual Themes is a much needed reference for group work with clients of all ages whose lives will be greatly enriched through discussions that deepen spiritual awareness. Promotion of spirituality through use of the book by health professionals will influence health care through engendering in people's lives a sense of hope and faith in the future.

Sister Rose Therese Bahr, A.S.C., Ph.D., R.N., F.A.A.N
Former Chair, American Nurses Association
Council of Gerontological Nursing

©1995 Whole Person Press 210 W Michigan Duluth MN 55802   (800) 247-6789

Hope is an act of collaboration; it cannot be achieved alone. We offer grains or fragments of hope to one another so that everyone's sense of possibility can grow. In this way we can do together what might seem impossible alone.

This book is such a gift of hope. It is rooted in the vision of human wholeness held by staff members at Sacred Heart Medical Center. This vision encompasses not only the physical and psychological aspects of the person, but those deeper questions and concerns which drive the human search for meaning—love, loss, judgement, guilt, forgiveness, faith. It integrates spirituality into the healing process, and is built on trust in the power of groups to promote the healing of their members.

This book is realistic and practical. Its authors offer the fruits of their own experience: guidelines for leading the group, a definition of spirituality that respects individual differences, creative exercises that can be duplicated or adapted to different audiences, and suggestions for responding to problems that might arise. It is evident throughout that they are presenting a process carefully developed and refined over time.

When I first met several of the staff at Sacred Heart Medical Center in the fall of 1989, I sensed that their care for their patients had a special quality to it. They were dedicated to a search for fresh visions and methods that would offer their patients as full an experience of themselves and the world as possible. I am happy that this book will now make the fruits of their enthusiasm and creativity available to other caring professionals.

Kathleen Fischer, Ph.D.
Seattle University
Author/Theologian/Counselor

©1995 Whole Person Press 210 W Michigan Duluth MN 55802   (800) 247-6789

TABLE OF CONTENTS

©1995 Whole Person Press 210 W Michigan Duluth MN 55802   (800) 247-6789

©1995 Whole Person Press 210 W Michigan Duluth MN 55802   (800) 247-6789

©1995 Whole Person Press 210 W Michigan Duluth MN 55802　　　　(800) 247-6789

INTRODUCTION

Spiritual awareness groups were developed over the course of several years by the staff of Main East of Sacred Heart Medical Center in Spokane, Washington, and now are an integral part of the Center's program. Our first experience showed us that people welcomed the opportunity to share their spiritual insights and wisdom in a group setting.

The original spiritual awareness group manual was developed by capturing the ongoing experiences of leaders and participants and combining them with research in the field of group work and spirituality.

This volume, *Working with Groups on Spiritual Themes*, builds on the original work, but expands the application to a wide variety of audiences in a multitude of settings. In fact, other spiritual awareness groups have been started based on this model, and leaders as well as participants have reported high satisfaction and excellent results. They, too, have found meaning and growth as they explored spiritual themes together. We have found that all of the concepts and exercises can be applied to groups and individuals in a wide range of settings.

As it has evolved the spiritual awareness group has typically been a one-hour weekly session with a focus on open discussion of spiritual issues.

Why have these groups been so successful? Too often, there is little time or attention paid to the spiritual aspect of our lives in our fast paced society. Using a group format to explore spiritual issues provides time for participants to reflect on various life themes and to search for meaning and purpose. It provides the opportunity for an individual to affirm a sense of community by sharing beliefs, values, and needs with others.

The spirituality group is a time for participants to discover sources of inner strength, and, ultimately, a place to find hope. Additionally, spirituality groups acknowledge the wholeness of body, mind, emotions, and spirit, and permit an opportunity for expression of the spiritual aspects of our nature. The group format provides affirmation and validation that an individual cannot receive alone.

And please don't think it's just the participants who benefit. Our experience indicates that leaders learn a whole lot about themselves and their own spiritual issues as they guide the discussions and listen to insights. So, don't be surprised if you soon discover that you're looking forward to the spiritual awareness group as a highlight of your week.

©1995 Whole Person Press 210 W Michigan Duluth MN 55802   (800) 247-6789

This book, *Working with Groups on Spiritual Themes*, reflects the dedicated work of the staff and the openness and courage of the group participants. It is our hope that the information provided here will generate the same enlightening experience for both professionals and participants everywhere that we have experienced over the years.

It is essential, we believe, that the spiritual dimension of health be included and nurtured, within the context of health care. To that goal we dedicate this effort.

Elaine Hopkins, R.N., C.
Zo Woods, R.N., B.S.N.
Russell Kelley, R.N., C.
Katrina Bentley, R.N., Ph.D.
James Murphy, M.A., Chaplain

April, 1995

©1995 Whole Person Press 210 W Michigan Duluth MN 55802   (800) 247-6789

Section I
Working with Spiritual Awareness Groups

Leaders of spiritual awareness groups find both challenge and
satisfaction in the process of helping people discover spiritual
depth. The information in this section will help you prepare
effectively to meet the challenge.

WORKING WITH
SPIRITUAL AWARENESS GROUPS

ADAPTING THE SESSIONS TO YOUR GROUP

A typical 60-75 minute spiritual awareness group session consists of three segments:

- Introduction/Warm-up (5-10 minutes)
- Theme discussion exercise (30-45 minutes)
- Closure (5-15 minutes)

You can easily adjust the timing to fit your audience and your content by condensing or lengthening the time allotted for discussion.

This book contains all the resources you need to conduct the group. The exercises in Section III present a wide variety of themes, and are outlined step-by-step to minimize your preparation time. Supplementary processes in Section II offer additional activities for the warm-up and closure portions of each session.

SPIRITUAL AWARENESS EXERCISES

The 39 spiritual awareness exercises in Section III of this book are geared for use with ongoing weekly discussion groups. The processes are outlined for sessions of 60 minutes each.

When you use the exercises with groups that are not ongoing, or that meet less frequently, you will want to incorporate one of the warm-up introductory processes from Section II into your session design.

Each spiritual awareness exercise serves as a guide for the group session. Some exercises provide a variety of ways in which the discussion can be conducted. It is important to emphasize that, while some discussions will need to be structured, other group sessions will generate free-flowing discussion and will require less structured leadership.

To meet the needs of all the group members, themes are as broadly based as possible and are not rooted in any particular religious tradition. For example, for the purposes of most groups, it is more effective to introduce a theme about God than one about Jesus Christ.

The theme focuses on experience rather than doctrine. Themes assist the participants in exploring and expanding their views on a variety of issues within a spiritual context. Themes are concrete rather than abstract or speculative. A constant effort is maintained to respect participants' unique and diverse experience.

©1995 Whole Person Press 210 W Michigan Duluth MN 55802   (800) 247-6789

Each exercise outlines the purpose, identifies resources needed, and gives specific instructions for conducting the session. Many exercises contain suggestions for alternative uses or ways to enhance the session. Some exercises contain worksheets and handouts.

You should feel free to apply your individual creativity in adapting the exercises to meet the needs of your audience and setting.

HOW TO PREPARE FOR LEADING THE GROUP

Although the steps in preparation for leading a spiritual awareness group are similar to those for any workshop or class you may teach, here are some thoughts to keep in mind that relate specifically to designing the spiritual group.

Preparing your session design

1. From Section III, select the spiritual awareness exercise you wish to use for the session. Read it several times and outline the steps so that you have a feel for the process.

   Note: For an ongoing group you may wish to ask participants to choose the theme for each session (in advance, of course). This encourages them to

---

DEFINITIONS

The terms "spirituality" and "religion" are often used interchangeably but they are not identical.

Spirituality is the way we orient ourselves toward the Divine. It is the way we make meaning out of our lives. It is the recognition of the presence of Spirit within us and a cultivation of a style of life consistent with that presence. Spirituality provides a perspective to foster purpose, meaning, and direction to life. It may find expressions through religion.*

Religion is a system of beliefs, values, rules for conduct, and rituals. It is a way a person's spirituality is expressed. Ideally, religion provides an atmosphere for spiritual development.†

Life Meanings relate to the significance an individual attributes to the events in his or her life within a spiritual context.

Life Issues include the continuum of problems or difficulties an individual faces such as death, tragedy, or impersonal losses.

*McBrien, R. P. 1981. Catholicism. Minneapolis: Winston Press.

† Carson, V. B. 1989. Spiritual dimensions of nursing practice. Philadelphia: W.B. Saunders Company. Used by permission.

---

take responsibility and feel ownership of their group. You then select an exercise that deals with the theme and build your session around it.

2. If you wish, select a supplementary process from Section II to help you open or close the session or stimulate additional discussion throughout.

3. Clearly outline in exact minutes the time table you imagine for the session. You won't want to hold to this schedule rigidly. However, you must have an idea of your timing so when it changes you will know whether you are ahead or behind your schedule, and you can quickly decide what to add or drop.

Preparing yourself

1. Answer all questions and complete all worksheets yourself. Make note of your own insights and personal examples. This will enrich the quality of the commentary you will bring to the teaching moment.

2. Think through the issues yourself and take them to heart. If the subject will be healing for others, it offers you that same opportunity.

3. Prior to the session, sit quietly and focus yourself, so that your mind and heart are connected and you feel calm and peaceful. There's something ironic, not to mention dysfunctional, for a leader to rush in at the last minute and frantically start to lead a group on spiritual awareness. So, get there early. Be sure that the room is ready and everything you need is at hand. Then, relax, focus yourself, and warmly greet the participants as they arrive.

Preparing the setting

1. Be sure that you have a chalkboard or easel paper available for the session. Recording summaries or highlights of the discussion provides visual reinforcement and recognizes contributions by the participants. The use of the chalkboard improves participants' concentration, helps to clarify thinking, assists in generating further ideas, and provides a means of redirecting focus. It is useful for creating worksheet summaries, group poetry, words of wisdom, and for recording definitions. We recommend that the chalkboard be available even if it is not specifically recommended for the scheduled exercise.

2. Handouts and worksheets that provide direction to the group discussion and that can be used by the participants for recording responses are provided with some exercises. Photocopy these materials prior to the session for distribution to the participants.

3. Certain props may be indicated for use with specific exercises. They are tools used to evoke recollection and discussion. When working with confused or cognitively impaired participants, props serve to help stimulate discussion among group members and encourage contact with reality.

   Props should be placed in the center of the room, easily visible to all members of the group. When they are used in the session, encourage participants to hold, touch, and pass the objects around the circle.

   You may wish to select a symbol such as a lighted candle to be a part of each session.

4. Arrange the seating in a close, informal circle. This promotes the feeling of togetherness and encourages sharing. Sitting at tables is not recommended, since they tend to separate people and create a formal classroom atmosphere not conducive to spiritual reflection and sharing. Focus on establishing a warm, informal, comfortable atmosphere.

LEADING THE GROUP PROCESS

The opening and introduction

At the beginning of each group session the following points should be addressed: group purpose, session theme, discussion guidelines, and confidentiality.

It is important that you take time to establish the purpose of the group and to provide for a safe, nonthreatening, trusting, objective environment for the expression of diverse views. Recognition can be made at this time if a member has contributed a centerpiece. It is appropriate to acknowledge members absent from the meeting and to introduce any new members. You might begin with comments similar to the following:

My name is _____, and I would like to welcome you to this spiritual awareness group. This is a time to come together to share beliefs, values, experiences, and the wisdom you have acquired over the years. Please feel comfortable in sharing what you believe, the sources of truth you embrace, and the values you hold dear.

The purpose of this group is to lift one another up, to encourage and affirm common values and experiences, and to honor those areas of difference. Your participation in various churches or other places of worship is welcome information, just as your lack of any particular religious affiliation is respected.

©1995 Whole Person Press 210 W Michigan Duluth MN 55802   (800) 247-6789

By sharing with other people your spiritual anchors and struggles, you can gain encouragement, enrichment, and wisdom. Information shared in this group is confidential and is not to be discussed with others outside this setting. This session will last for one hour.

In a moment I will ask that you introduce yourself by the name you like to be called. I will also begin with a warm-up question to help start the discussion and to help us get to know something about each other.

The theme of this session will be _____.

The process exercise and the discussion

Each exercise introduces the topic and identifies the key question for the session. An additional list of open-ended discussion questions is provided for most exercises. Don't get too task oriented and try to plow through all of these questions in a hurry. They are tough questions that will stimulate deep thinking.

Responses to questions provide a starting point. It is important that you carefully listen to the responses and remain flexible. Sometimes the group members may benefit from further exploration of a question rather than proceeding to the next question. Ask for feedback using such phrases as:

- Does anyone else have anything to share about this?

- Before we move on, is there anything more to discuss about this?

- That was an interesting comment. Could you explain more?

Remember, the quality of the discussion is what's important—not getting through all of the questions. So, always ask the group first for insights and observations about the worksheet, activity, or reading, before asking additional questions. Then, listen and follow the conversation that occurs. Accept what people say and summarize what you hear. Let people struggle with the concept and explore their own, and each other's thinking on the issue. Encourage everyone to participate. As people share with and listen to each other, new insights will emerge. Trust the process and give it time.

Sometimes you will want to move the discussion along by raising questions about aspects of the issue that the group may be neglecting. Some groups will need more prodding, depending on their insight level and their willingness to share with each other. That's the purpose of the additional

©1995 Whole Person Press 210 W Michigan Duluth MN 55802   (800) 247-6789

ADDITIONAL TIPS FOR LEADING DISCUSSION

- If your group is large, you can maximize the effectiveness of the discussion time by dividing the group into smaller units of 4–5 people. People get more time to share their ideas in the smaller groups.

- Listen and be involved. Your energy, enthusiasm, and comfort is transferred to the members and effectively enhances group participation.

- Keep in mind that it is not necessary to have all the answers. Honesty, support, empathy, and appreciation reinforce the self-worth, value, and meaning for group participants.

- Avoid probing into the particularly difficult or painful experiences of members, but give support as these experiences are recalled and addressed.

- Expand on, rather than explain members' contributions.

- Use open-ended questions.

- Guide the group members from a superficial to a more personal and deeper level of experience, by asking, "How does that affect you personally? Can you give me an example."

- Encourage group members to respond to each others' contributions.

- Emphasize the threads of common feelings and experiences.

- Be alert for the need to redirect the group back to the central theme or issue and to periodically summarize the members' contributions and the themes that have emerged.

- Encourage the members to bring comfort items, such as sweaters or a beverage, to the group.

- Offer support to members who need assistance in getting to the group.

- Set firm but gentle limits on inappropriate monopolizing behavior.

- Long pauses and periods of silence can be characteristic of a group. Allow this as a time for thought and reflection. Do not rush the discussion.

- When possible, encourage members to write or tape record memories, poems, or sayings outside of group sessions. Use the creative talents of members in the group session.

- Encourage members to take increased roles of responsibility for each other and for the discussion.

- In making the seating arrangements, consider the sensory impairments of the participants, allowing those members who are hard of hearing to sit next to you. Also try to seat yourself next to potentially excessive talkers. You can redirect them more easily when you are nearby.

questions. Look them over ahead of time so that you can personalize each question and ask it in your own words. Remember to keep the questions open-ended so that they elicit a give-and-take discussion rather than a search for right answers. The purpose is to stimulate discussion. People learn the most when they explore ideas with each other. If the conversation is going well, don't stop the process by throwing in more questions than are needed. It's OK to save a few for another session.

It may be necessary for you to gently limit the time taken for individual responses to questions so that all the members can participate. At times it would be appropriate to encourage a participant to speak longer (for example, when the individual is working through a deep grief and loss or during a spiritual crisis), but the recommended limit for most discussions is two or three minutes per person.

Remember, you do not need to be a theologian. You are not required to have all the answers. In fact, your job is to be an empathic, supportive, and flexible listener, not to be the judge of right or wrong, good or evil.

The closing

Always allow ample time to close the session in a positive manner by summarizing important aspects of participants' contributions and by encouraging and assisting the participants to set goals and to follow through on them. Give individuals positive feedback and affirmation for their contributions. Say "thank you." You might wish to vary your closure process with the following ideas.

- Read a brief meditation or poem.

- Hold a group prayer (only with the permission of all).

- Provide a quiet time and silence.

- Ask each participant to express gratitude for something that occurred during the session.

- Invite people to encourage each other in reaching the goals they have set for themselves.

- Provide prizes, mementos, or posters as take-home reinforcers of the session's theme.

- Ask the group how they would like to close the experience and follow their lead.

THE EVALUATION

Once participants leave the session, you, as leader, still have one responsibility remaining—evaluate the process. Hold a debriefing session with
yourself (or your partner if you have a coleader). It is helpful if you write
a summary of your reflections in your log book for future reference. Think
about the following issues:

- What were the signals from each participant? Were they involved?
  withdrawn? Does anyone need special guidance or encouragement at
  the next session? or immediately?

- What questions and responses seemed most helpful or least helpful in
  fostering the group process?

- What changes would be helpful in the future?

- What issues that surfaced need follow-up in either individual sessions
  or future group sessions?

- Did any new themes emerge that should be further developed?

- Did you as the leader at any point get emotionally involved and forget
  to listen well? Did you miss any key signals from the group or from
  individual members?

                              ****

In the next two sections, you will find supplemental group processes and
the spiritual awareness exercises. Use them creatively. Don't be afraid to
adapt them as necessary. And—enjoy the experience of leading the
spiritual awareness group. All people, ourselves included, are on a similar
pilgrimage. We leaders have as much to learn in these discussions as our
participants.

Section II
Supplementary Group Processes

The 39 spiritual awareness exercises in Section III deal with huge concepts such as trust, grief, hope, honesty, values, wonder, wisdom, and creativity. The purpose of the spiritual awareness group is to help people reflect on subjects that sometimes seem to be abstract concepts and to bring these concepts to life for each participant.

The content and process for each exercise is outlined completely and can be used just as presented. However, discussing spiritual concepts can be a difficult task. Therefore, at times you will want to vary the activity and the rhythm of your sessions to help people expand a concept, to encourage sharing, and to stimulate a more lively discussion.

The nine supplemental process ideas outlined in this section will help you increase the level of creativity and energy generated by the spiritual awareness discussion exercises. As you plan your session, select the process that you feel will best fit the subject and the needs, interests, and comfort level of your group. Session by session, vary the processes to help your group maintain a consistently high level of energy.

SUPPLEMENTARY PROCESSES

QUICK QUESTIONS   (p 13)

This stimulating process helps participants meet each other and begin sharing ideas. It helps relieve first session tension and promotes lively interaction.

QUIETING VISUALIZATION   (p 15)

This guided meditation process helps set a quiet, thoughtful tone for the session.

WORD WISDOM   (p 16)

This brief brainstorming process offers a method for identifying the phrases and meanings that participants connect with a specific word or topic.

WORD FLOWER   (p 17)

This activity helps the group creatively expand the range of images associated with a core word or topic.

MODELS AND HEROES   (p 19)

This exercise helps participants discover specific characteristics of a spiritual concept by identifying a person who exemplifies the concept and summarizing that person's positive qualities.

FAVORITE SAYINGS   (p 20)

Participants recall and explain the meaning of favorite sayings or verses that relate to the topic.

KEY EXPERIENCES   (p 21)

Participants recall a specific life experience that relates to the topic. They identify the wisdom they gained from that event and apply it to the present.

GROUP POETRY   (p 22)

Participants summarize the key images and concepts of a discussion by creating a poem that captures the feelings and thoughts of their group.

JOURNALING   (p 23)

Participants continue the development of their insights about a specific topic or feeling by recording their thoughts, feelings, and experiences in a daily journal.

QUICK QUESTIONS

This stimulating process helps participants meet each other and begin sharing ideas. It helps relieve first session tension and promotes lively interaction.

PROCESS

☞ *Before the session begins, select a sequence of 6–8 questions that relate to the topic of the session. Make them interesting, surprising, and meaningful. Use only open-ended (story-telling) questions, never ones that can be answered "yes" or "no." Use the sample questions at the end of this description, or make up your own.*

1. Ask everyone in the group to stand, to move around the room, and to select a partner. (Be sure everyone has found a partner before proceeding.)

2. Ask your first question. Instruct participants to introduce themselves to each other and share a short answer to the question. Allow 2 minutes for this.

3. Interrupt and instruct people to move and find a new partner. Sometimes you may want to increase the mix by asking people to move across the room before selecting their next partner.

4. Repeat steps 2 and 3 for four or five sequences. Then, ask participants to return to their seats. Encourage comments, then introduce the topic of the session.

NOTES AND SUGGESTIONS

- This process is best used at the first session as a get acquainted mixer, but it can also be very effective when used as an energizing opening to a topic-focused session.

- Be sure to select a sequence of questions that, on the one hand, are not too threatening, but, on the other hand, get at the heart of the session topic. Questions that provoke laughter or slight embarrassment often add a bit of humor and fun.

- Usually four or five rounds of questions will be enough.

- Keep the process moving quickly, spending only 2–3 minutes on each question. Then interrupt, change partners, and ask a new question.

QUICK SAMPLE QUESTIONS

Select a series of questions from the list that follows, or develop one that is appropriate to your group:

✔ What is special about you?

✔ Which is your favorite season of the year? Why?

✔ What is the best advice you ever received?

✔ If you had two wishes, what would they be?

✔ If you could give any gift in the world, what would you give to the person you are introducing yourself to?

✔ What is your favorite inspirational song?

✔ What is your favorite room in your house? Why?

✔ What is your nickname or pet name? Who gave you that name?

✔ What two things are most important in your life?

✔ What color do you think of when you think of happiness?

✔ What one quality do you look for most in friends?

✔ Whom do you admire most? In what way does that person inspire you?

✔ What does the world most need?

✔ What do you like most about yourself?

✔ What is the most sentimental possession that you have?

✔ If you had to move and could take only three things with you, what would you take?

✔ What do you like best about your life?

✔ If you were to add spice to life, what would it be and why?

✔ What is your most spiritual body part? Describe it.

QUIETING VISUALIZATION

This guided meditation process helps set a quiet, thoughtful tone for the session.

PROCESS

1. Introduce the subject for the session. Tell participants that you will provide a few minutes of quiet time at the beginning of the session for them to consider what this topic (or word) means to them and the images they connect with it.

2. Encourage participants to relax and get comfortable, to close their eyes and get quiet inside, to take three slow deep breaths, and to consider the meaning of the topic and the images that come to mind. During the quiet you may suggest questions or images for consideration. (5-10 minutes)

3. Gently, warn the participants that you will soon be asking them to return their attention to the room. Repeat this information two or three times if necessary until all participants open their eyes and appear ready to move on.

4. Ask for feedback about the experience, then move on to the spiritual awareness exercise.

NOTES AND SUGGESTIONS

- Make sure the room is quiet and comfortable.

- You may wish to play soft background music and turn the lights down. (Don't turn them completely off.)

- Take your time in step 2. Don't rush the process. Let the quiet take over. Trust that the quiet is full of images. It will be.

- Be careful not to end the process too abruptly. Give people a minute or two to return their focus to the room.

©1995 Whole Person Press 210 W Michigan Duluth MN 55802   (800) 247-6789

WORD WISDOM

This brief brainstorming process offers a method for identifying the phrases and meanings that participants connect with a specific word or topic.

MATERIALS

Chalk and chalkboard.

PROCESS

☞ *This exercise can be used as a brief way of obtaining a definition of the issue that will be explored. It is also a way for the leader to ascertain the participants' perspective on the topic.*

1. Write the topic word followed by "is" on the chalkboard. Ask the participants to add the endings. The suggestions are recorded on the chalkboard. Elicit as many responses as possible and write them all on the chalkboard.

   For example: Honesty is _____.

2. Ask the group to reflect on the list they have generated and to share their observations and reactions.

3. Continue with the rest of the spiritual awareness exercise you are using for this session.

NOTES AND SUGGESTIONS

- Be sure to record every suggestion. This is a brainstorming process. All answers are "correct." All should be accepted and recorded.

- You may wish to type and photocopy the group's list and distribute it to them.

©1995 Whole Person Press 210 W Michigan Duluth MN 55802   (800) 247-6789

WORD FLOWER

This activity helps the group creatively expand the range of images associated with a core word or topic.

MATERIALS

Chalk and chalkboard; paper; pens or pencils.

PROCESS

1. Place the topic word for the session (for example, Spirituality, Peace, Love, Heaven, Honor, Care) inside a circle drawn on the chalkboard.

2. Ask the participants to share all the words they associate with the word in the circle. Add those words as petals on the flower.

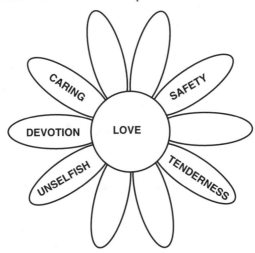

Add words around the word in the circle until all the petals are filled.

3. Ask the participants to select one of the words for further discussion. Lead the discussion by asking participants to describe specifics: Who? How? When? Where? What? Why? Record highlights of the discussion on the chalkboard.

©1995 Whole Person Press 210 W Michigan Duluth MN 55802   (800) 247-6789

4. In closing, summarize the highlights of the discussion and connect common experiences that were shared. Then, continue with the spiritual awareness exercise.

NOTES AND SUGGESTIONS

- This exercise can be used as a focus process to obtain quick information about participants' spiritual perspectives or about thoughts associated with a selected topic.

MODELS AND HEROES

This exercise helps participants discover specific characteristics of a spiritual concept by identifying a person who exemplifies the concept and summarizing that person's positive qualities.

MATERIALS

Paper; pens or pencils.

PROCESS

1. Introduce the topic of the session.

2. Distribute a sheet of paper to each participant. Ask them to identify a person who exemplifies the best of the session's theme (for example, maturity, wisdom, or hope). The person each participant chooses can be living or dead, family, friend, or stranger. Participants write the person's name on their paper.

3. Ask participants to write a short statement about their selected person, highlighting the qualities they most admire.

4. Encourage participants to share the name of the person they selected and two or three qualities they admire. Keep this moving quickly. Simply get a list of the qualities and write them on the chalkboard.

5. Ask the group to look over the list of qualities on the chalkboard and reflect on how well the list fits with the topic for the session.

NOTES AND SUGGESTIONS

• This process can be used for almost any subject as a way of helping participants personally identify with the topic.

• In step 4 people may want to tell complete stories about the person they chose. Encourage them, rather, to just list the qualities and move on. This process, when used as a warm-up should be relatively brief (10-15 minutes total).

FAVORITE SAYINGS

Participants recall and explain the meaning of favorite sayings or verses that relate to the topic.

MATERIALS

Paper; pens or pencils.

PROCESS

1. Introduce the topic of the session.

2. Ask participants to recall and write down a favorite saying related to the topic. The phrase might be something they learned in childhood, an old maxim, or an advertising slogan.

3. Point out that most favorite sayings contain strong messages. Ask participants to reflect on the message of their saying and to share with the group the point that the phrase is trying to teach.

4. Summarize and comment on the variety and richness of information and beliefs about the topic that have surfaced, pointing out that the group already knows a lot about the subject.

NOTES AND SUGGESTIONS

- Additional questions you might ask could include:
  - ✔ Where or how did you learn this verse?
  - ✔ Who taught you this verse? Describe the person.
  - ✔ How can you expand on these verses?
  - ✔ How have you applied this verse to your life?
  - ✔ In what way does this verse or saying bring you closer to an awareness of your spirituality?

©1995 Whole Person Press 210 W Michigan Duluth MN 55802   (800) 247-6789

KEY EXPERIENCES

Participants recall a specific life experience that relates to the topic. They identify the wisdom they gained from that event and apply it to the present.

MATERIALS

Chalk and chalkboard; paper; pens or pencils.

PROCESS

1. Introduce the topic of the session.

2. Distribute a sheet of paper to each participant. Ask them to recall and write on the paper a time in their life when they dealt with the issue. For example, if the topic is hope, ask:

   ✔ When did you feel hopeless?

   ✔ When have you felt most hopeful?

3. Instruct participants to recall all aspects of the experience and to make notes on the circumstances:

   ✔ Where were you?

   ✔ How old were you?

   ✔ What was going on in your life at the time?

   ✔ How were you feeling?

4. Ask participants to summarize their reflections by writing a statement that reflects the overall tone and mood of their experience.

5. As participants share their statements, summarize them on the chalkboard.

6. Encourage the sharing of reflections and comments about the group's compiled list. Then, proceed with the spiritual awareness exercise.

NOTES AND SUGGESTIONS

- Some participants may have recalled an experience of great pain. Encourage them to share only their summary statement. If you allow them to tell the whole story, you may take the entire session for this process. There's nothing wrong with that, of course, if that's your plan. Otherwise keep it focused and moving quickly.

©1995 Whole Person Press 210 W Michigan Duluth MN 55802   (800) 247-6789

GROUP POETRY

Participants summarize the key images and concepts of a discussion by creating a poem that captures the feelings and thoughts of their group.

MATERIALS

Paper; pens or pencils.

PROCESS

1. Form groups of 4–5 persons. Ask them to summarize the main themes that have emerged during the session (5 minutes).

2. From this summary, instruct them to write a poem about these themes that reflects the feelings and experiences of the group. (10 minutes).

3. Reconvene the group and ask each small group to read their poem to the rest of the group.

4. If time allows, encourage the entire group to create a single, unified poem utilizing the creations of all.

NOTES AND SUGGESTIONS

- This process works best as a way to draw together insights and close the session with a celebration.

- Let the participants know that they have 10 minutes. Keep the momentum going. People can be wonderfully creative when under time pressure.

- You may want to type and photocopy the poems, then distribute copies to the group at the next session.

©1995 Whole Person Press 210 W Michigan Duluth MN 55802   (800) 247-6789

JOURNALING

Participants continue the development of their insights about a specific topic or feeling by recording their thoughts, feelings, and experiences in a daily journal.

MATERIALS

Paper; pens or pencils.

PROCESS

1. Discuss the purpose of the exercise: to learn how to record events, the meaning of these events, and how you feel about things that happen in your life, as presented in the **Guidelines for Journaling**.

2. Present the material in the **Guidelines for Journaling**, printed at the end of this exercise, condensing or expanding on this material as time allows.

3. Distribute paper and guide participants in the use of a feelings journal, asking them to review today's events and list in a column on the left side of the page everything they did throughout the day.

4. In preparation for the next step in this process define the word "feelings."

   - Feelings are positive or negative emotions, such as joy, euphoria, neutrality, anxiety, sadness, or fear.

   - Feelings are short lived (as opposed to moods, like depression, which are longer lasting).

   - The event or events that led to a feeling can usually be identified.

   - Feelings are a measure of the quality of our lives: the more people experience positive feelings, the higher the quality of their lives.

   - Feelings provide us with information and can be indicators of things in our life that may need to be changed.

5. Instruct participants to describe on the right side of the page the feelings that accompanied each event of the day.

6. Emphasize that the journaling process is used to provide a safe and private place to express one's emotional life. Any type of record can be used (a loose leaf or spiral bound notebook, tape recorder, etc.).

7. Encourage participants to try to keep a daily record of events, thoughts, and feelings. Suggest that they periodically review their journal entries to assess their own growth.

NOTES AND SUGGESTIONS

- This process is a powerful tool for encouraging continued learning outside the session.

- This process can be the topic for an entire session focused on training in the art of journaling, or it can be used as a 15-20 minute closing reflection as presented here.

©1995 Whole Person Press 210 W Michigan Duluth MN 55802   (800) 247-6789

GUIDELINES FOR JOURNALING

Journaling is a way of recording thoughts, feelings, and experiences for review at a later time. It provides a safe and private place to express one's emotional life. Journals often become powerful reflective tools and help a person trace individual progress in the development of insight and the resolution of issues.

Reasons for journaling

1. To record thoughts, feelings, or experiences.
2. To express thoughts and feelings in a way that is both private and safe.
3. To develop insight into the meaning of life events within the context of personal experience.
4. To reflect on progress and growth by recording events, thoughts, and feelings as they occur.
5. To resolve issues such as grief, loss, and traumatic events in a safe outlet for the expression of thoughts and feelings.
6. To record goals that have been set and how well those goals have been met.

Types of journals

The format of the journal may be individualized to meet the person's unique needs. Some common methods for maintaining journals include:

1. Writing a daily log or record of events, thoughts, and feelings. If the individual has difficulty writing, another person may serve as a recorder.
2. Audiotaping thoughts and feelings.
3. Videotaping special events.
4. Photographing people and events. (The family photo album is, in reality, a picture journal of a family's life together.)
5. Developing a computer file of events and thoughts. Computers are particularly useful tools for writers with handicaps.

©1995 Whole Person Press 210 W Michigan Duluth MN 55802   (800) 247-6789

Types of journal entries

The content of journal entries may be focused in one of several ways:

1. Activity or event oriented: The focus is on what happened, the circumstances, the persons involved.

2. Process oriented: Only basic details of an event are recorded. The focus is on the meaning of the event and the journal writer's thoughts and feelings about the event.

3. Feelings oriented: The central theme is how the individual is feeling internally or in relation to others.

How to use a journal

1. Use a notebook or a durable blank book so that the journal is easy to keep.

2. Date each journal entry and use ink and legible printing or handwriting. Oral journals may be made on cassette tape by individuals not physically able to write or who express themselves better this way.

3. Use a variety of entry formats, but try to include feelings and process as much as possible. Writing only about events is dry and meaningless journaling.

4. Ideally, a daily entry in the journal is best, but this may not be practical. Journalers should be encouraged to use the journal as a mirror to reflect their concerns and progress. The journal writing schedule should not become so rigid that the journal loses its value.

5. The use of a focused, sentence-completion type of journal format is helpful for starters.

Section III
Spiritual Awareness Exercises

Growing Spiritually

People engaged on a spiritual quest want to explore serious topics such as faith and the meaning of life. They also have practical concerns such as how to find peace during difficult times. The exercises in this section help people find their own answers to tough questions.

GROWING SPIRITUALLY

1 SPIRITUAL ASSESSMENT (p 29)

Using a worksheet followed by discussion, participants examine their own spiritual issues and needs.

2 SPIRITUALITY (p 32)

Participants discuss their past and present spirituality and begin to set goals for leading a more spiritual life.

3 FAITH (p 33)

Participants define faith, describe the value and benefits of faith, and identify and record ways to strengthen faith and its application in life.

4 MEANING AND PURPOSE (p 36)

Participants explore meaning and purpose in life, considering the changes that take place over a lifetime.

5 PEACE (p 39)

Participants explore the experience of peace and develop plans to bring peace into their lives.

6 PEACE DURING ADVERSITY (p 41)

Using discussion and poetry, participants develop ways to experience peace in difficult times.

7 HOPE VERSUS DESPAIR (p 43)

Through group discussion and poetry, participants identify sources of hope and discover ways to decrease feelings of hopelessness.

8 GOD'S PRESENCE (p 45)

Participants identify the presence or absence of God in their lives and discuss ways that they may increase their awareness of that presence.

1 SPIRITUAL ASSESSMENT

Using a worksheet followed by discussion, participants examine their own spiritual issues and needs.

MATERIALS

Pens or pencils; **Spiritual Assessment** worksheet.

☞ *Prior to asking people to join a spirituality group, counselors may want to conduct personal interviews using the questions from the **Spiritual Assessment** worksheet.*

PROCESS

1. Introduce the goals of the exercise:
   - To consider the following issues: a philosophy of life, sources of hope, trusting relationships, and self-actualization
   - To recognize that many people struggle with similar questions
   - To help leaders understand the concerns and needs of the group

2. Distribute the **Spiritual Assessment** worksheet and allow participants about 20 minutes to complete it.

   ☞ *If you plan to collect the worksheets at the end of the session, advise participants of this before they begin work.*

   The questions are broad and far-ranging. Encourage participants to read all the questions first, then to begin answering those that interest them the most. There's no need for them to answer every question completely. Be sure, however, that everyone completes the last question before time is up.

3. Ask participants to share their reactions with each other and to comment on the following questions:

   ✔ Which questions did you find particularly difficult to answer?

   ✔ Which questions challenged you to think about your future?

   ✔ What issues would you like to discuss in this spirituality group?

4. Conclude the exercise by stating that the concerns people have mentioned will be addressed in the next sessions.

SPIRITUAL ASSESSMENT

Name: _____

What is important to you in your life right now? _____

_____

_____

What was important to you in the past? _____

_____

_____

What does growing older mean to you? _____

_____

Do you consider yourself to be young or old? _____

Do you think your life has become better or worse as you have grown

older? _____

Why? _____

_____

Do you expect your life to be better or worse in the future? _____

_____

When you're discouraged or feeling hopeless, what keeps you going?

_____

_____

Where have you found strength in the past? _____

_____

Do you believe in a power greater than yourself? _____

Who or what is it? _____

_____

Do you feel more like being alone or with other people right now?

_____

©1995 Whole Person Press 210 W Michigan Duluth MN 55802   (800) 247-6789

How much control do you believe you have over what happens to you in your life? _____

_____

Do you have a personal means for meeting your inner spiritual needs? (For example, prayer or scripture reading.) _____

_____

What do you believe happens to you when you die? _____

_____

_____

Has this made a difference in how you have lived your life? _____

_____

_____

What are your special creative abilities? _____

_____

_____

What does beauty mean to you? _____

_____

What do you consider beautiful in the world? _____

_____

Look over your answers, then write a couple of observations and insights that occur to you about these questions and your answers. What do you notice? _____

_____

_____

_____

This Spiritual Assessment *is inspired by the work of Steven S. Ivy. Ivy based his assessment on the works of James Fowler, Robert Kegan, and the Constructivist/ Developmental Model of Psychology.*

©1995 Whole Person Press 210 W Michigan Duluth MN 55802   (800) 247-6789

2 SPIRITUALITY

Participants discuss their past and present spirituality and begin to set goals for leading a more spiritual life.

MATERIALS

Chalk and chalkboard; paper; pens or pencils.

PROCESS

1. Share the purpose of this session with your group. The following statements are possibilities:

   • To develop personal definitions of spirituality

   • To become aware of unique and common threads in spiritual beliefs

   • To begin planning to live a more spiritual life

2. Encourage participants to write their own definition of spirituality.

3. Ask participants to share their definitions with the group, recording responses on the chalkboard.

4. Ask the group to comment on these definitions. In addition, you may want to ask the following questions as time allows or post the questions and ask the group to select those they most want to discuss.

   ✔ Was there a time in your life that you were most aware of your sense of spirituality? When? What was it like? What happened?

   ✔ What role does God play in your definition of spirituality?

   ✔ Is your spirituality more or less important to you now than in the past? Why do you think this is true?

   ✔ How do you live a spiritual life or practice your spirituality now?

   ✔ What nourishes your sense of spirituality the most?

   ✔ How would you like to practice a more spiritual life now?

   ✔ What goals can you set to begin practicing a more spiritual life?

VARIATION

■ If additional time is available, the *Group Poetry* process in Section II of this book could be used.

3   FAITH

Participants define faith, describe the value and benefits of faith, and identify and record ways to strengthen faith and its application in life.

MATERIALS

Chalk and chalkboard; pens or pencils; **Faith** worksheet.

PROCESS

1. Distribute the worksheet and ask participants to write their own definition of faith in section 1.

   ☞ *While they are working, write the worksheet headings on the chalkboard, leaving plenty of room in each section for notes.*

2. Ask participants to share their definitions, and write their comments on the chalkboard.

3. Encourage participants to continue answering the questions on the worksheet, one section at a time. After they complete each section, take 5 minutes for discussion, noting their insights on the chalkboard. The following questions may help stimulate discussion:

   Section 2: What are the qualities of faith?

   ✔ Have you had a role model for your faith?

   ✔ What are or were the qualities of this person's faith?

   Section 3: How can we strengthen our faith?

   ✔ What persons or events have had the most impact in the development and strengthening of your faith?

   ✔ In what ways, if any, has your faith ever been shaken or tested?

   ✔ Has that experience strengthened or weakened your faith?

   ✔ What are your faith builders?

   Section 4: What are the benefits of faith?

   ✔ What has your faith given to you?

   Section 5: How does faith become evident in life?

   ✔ How have you demonstrated your faith in your life?

©1995 Whole Person Press 210 W Michigan Duluth MN 55802   (800) 247-6789

✔ What role will faith play in your future?

Section 6: My goals for the future.

✔ Are there specific goals you can set to strengthen the application of your faith, day by day?

4. As a closing process, invite individuals to share their goals for the future with each other.

5. Summarize the contributions made by participants and remind them that they, too, are role models, who can support and strengthen the faith of other family members and friends.

©1995 Whole Person Press 210 W Michigan Duluth MN 55802   (800) 247-6789

FAITH

1. What is faith?

2. What are the qualities of faith?

3. How can we strengthen our faith?

4. What are the benefits of faith?

5. How does faith become evident in life?

6. My goals for the future:

4   MEANING AND PURPOSE

Participants explore meaning and purpose in life, considering the changes that take place over a lifetime.

MATERIALS

Chalk and chalkboard; pens or pencils; selected readings on the topic; **Meaning and Purpose** worksheet.

PROCESS

1. Distribute the **Meaning and Purpose** worksheet and advise participants that they will be completing it one section at a time.

   ☞ *The worksheet may also be used with individuals, or to encourage additional reflection, it can be given to participants at the conclusion of discussion.*

2. Open the discussion by asking participants to complete sections 1 and 2 on the worksheet.

   ☞ *While they are working, write the worksheet headings on the chalkboard, leaving plenty of room in each section for notes.*

3. As participants share and discuss their responses to the worksheet sections, record their insights on the chalkboard.

4. Ask participants to complete section 3 of the worksheet, reflecting on their awareness of purpose and meaning in life as children, adolescents, young adults, mid-life adults, and older adults. As they discuss their ideas, record them on the chalkboard.

5. Ask participants to complete and then discuss section 4.

6. As time allows select questions from the list below that seem relevant:

   ✔ Is there purpose in life?

   ✔ What is the relationship between meaning and purpose?

   ✔ How have you discovered purpose and meaning in life?

   ✔ Have you helped other people discover their purpose or meaning? Describe that experience.

©1995 Whole Person Press 210 W Michigan Duluth MN 55802   (800) 247-6789

✔ In what ways have you fostered your sense of individual meaning and purpose?

✔ What do you believe is God's purpose for mankind in general? For you as an individual?

7. Ask participants to complete and then discuss section 5.

8. Provide several minutes for silent reflection. Conclude by asking participants to share their thoughts on ways in which they can foster and nurture the ongoing discovery of meaning and purpose.

VARIATION

■ Prior to the session, select one or more readings on life purpose that are meaningful to you and share them with the group as a meditation to close the session.

©1995 Whole Person Press 210 W Michigan Duluth MN 55802   (800) 247-6789

MEANING AND PURPOSE

1. Write your definition of meaning in life. What is meaningful to you?

2. Write your definition of purpose. What gives your life purpose?

3. Note the purpose you recall at various stages of your life.

Childhood _____

_____

Adolescence _____

_____

Young adult _____

_____

Mid-life _____

_____

Later life _____

_____

4. How do you discover purpose and meaning in your life?
   (List key events, discussions, crises, focusing moments.)

5. How can you continue to clarify your meaning and purpose?

5 PEACE

Participants explore the experience of peace and develop plans to bring peace into their lives.

MATERIALS

Prescription for Peace handout.

PROCESS

1. Help participants to recall a time when they experienced peace.

   ☞ *You may use the **Key Experiences** or the **Quieting Visualization** process in Section II of this book to do this.*

2. Ask participants to share their experiences and to discuss similarities and differences.

3. Lead a discussion using the following questions:

   ✔ What factors contributed to this sense of peace? Were you with a specific person, in a certain place, or involved in a particular activity?

   ✔ How do you feel when you are not at peace?

   ✔ How much control do you have over your sense of peace?

4. Distribute copies of the **Prescription for Peace** handout to everyone. After a volunteer reads it, ask participants to discuss the following questions:

   ✔ Which prescription is most meaningful to you?

   ✔ What can you do to experience more peace in your life?

5. In closing, with the permission of all the participants, ask each participant, in turn, to repeat the greeting "Peace be with you," while standing in a circle and joining hands.

©1995 Whole Person Press 210 W Michigan Duluth MN 55802   (800) 247-6789

Prescription for Peace

Forgive our parents totally.

Forgive everyone who has ever been here, who is here now,
or who will ever be here, including ourselves, totally.

Forgive the world totally.

Forgive God totally.

Take a leap in faith and trust in love, trust in God.

Choose to experience peace rather than conflict.

Choose to experience love rather than fear.

Choose to be a love finder rather than a fault finder.

Choose to be a love giver rather than a love seeker.

Teach only love.

                                        by Gerald G. Jampolsky, M.D.

6 PEACE DURING ADVERSITY

Using discussion and poetry, participants develop ways to experience peace in difficult times.

MATERIALS

The poem "The Secret."

PROCESS

1. Read the poem, "The Secret," as a meditation. Encourage people to relax, shut their eyes, and become quiet.

   ☞ The **Quieting Visualization** process in Section II of this book may help you prepare to lead groups through a visualization.

2. Ask participants what they believe the relationship is between having material wealth and having peace. The questions that follow might be used as discussion stimulators:

   ✔ Why do you think a poor person might be happy?

   ✔ Have you ever experienced poverty?

   ✔ If so, what experiences can you recall about being poor, in a material sense?

   ✔ Have you ever known anyone who was poor yet happy?

   ✔ What is the secret of happiness?

   ✔ What wisdom is in this happiness?

   ✔ Can you think of a time in your life when being grateful resulted in your personal experience of happiness?

   ✔ How can an individual experience peace in the midst of adversity?

3. Following the discussion, close the group by challenging each participant regularly to practice being grateful. Share an example of how they might do this today by saying:

   • You can be grateful and find peace right now.

   • Begin by saying "thank you" to each other for something that you appreciated during this session and notice the peace that begins to fill the room.

©1995 Whole Person Press 210 W Michigan Duluth MN 55802   (800) 247-6789

The Secret

I set out in search
of the source of happiness.
I look minutely at the life
of a happy person who is poor,
then talk with him, attempting to discover
what makes this person happy.
I think of a joyful person in poor health,
in physical pain,
and talk again, searching for what it is
that makes her joyful.
I do the same with a happy person
who has lost his reputation.
I walk into a prison
and am amazed to find a happy person even here.
She tells me what it is
that makes her happy.
                    ❧

Then I observe unhappy people who are free and wealthy,
powerful,
respectable.
I talk to them,
and as they talk to me
I listen carefully to their complaints.
                    ❧

Yesterday I had occasions to be happy
That I wasn't even conscious of.
I see them now.
It is inconceivable that anyone
could be grateful and unhappy.
I thank the Lord for each event of yesterday
and notice the effect this has on me.
And the things I call unpleasant, undesirable
—I search for the good that comes from these . . .
the seeds for growth they carry . . .
and find reason to be grateful for them too.
Finally I see myself
moving through each portion of today
in gratitude
—and happiness.

> *Reprinted from deMello, Anthony. 1985. The Secret.* Wellsprings: A book of
> spiritual exercises. *New York: Doubleday and Company.*

7 HOPE VERSUS DESPAIR

Through group discussion and poetry, participants identify sources of hope and discover ways to decrease feelings of hopelessness.

MATERIALS

Chalk and chalkboard; inspirational readings selected by participants.

PROCESS

☞ *Prior to the session, request that participants bring a favorite short inspirational reading to the session. (This may include favorite verses of poetry, words of wisdom, or Bible readings.) If this is not possible, bring a selection of your own favorites or use those on the next page.*

1. Ask participants to share one thing they feel hopeful about and to define the word "hope."

2. Use the following questions to foster discussion. (You may want to record highlights of the discussion on the chalkboard.)

   ✔ What does it mean to have hope?

   ✔ When life seems most discouraging or hopeless, what holds you up or renews your hope?

   ✔ When you think about the future, what makes you feel most anxious or uneasy?

   > For yourself?

   > For those you love?

   > For society in this country?

   > For the world?

   ✔ Does hope affect attitudes?

   ✔ Does hope affect health? How?

3. Ask participants to note what they are most hopeful about. Give them time to share their hopes with each other.

4. Discuss sources of hope and the connection between spiritual beliefs and practices in relation to hope.

5. Ask participants to describe ways they can support hope for others. Discuss the value of role modeling, prayer, support, kind deeds, and empathetic listening.

6. Discuss actions that participants can take that will create and foster a sense of hope within themselves.

7. In closing, ask participants to read several inspirational readings. Here are some samples other groups have used.

One Step Higher

When life goes wrong
And you seem to tire
Don't give up the ship
Take one step higher
It might be hard
With irons on fire
Don't give up yet
Take one step higher
If the bog is wide
And deep the mire
Keep up the struggle
And step up even higher

      by Dovie Lee Manning

The Light

The Light projects my way thru'
the Darkness.
The moonlight night.
The Light chases the shadows
from my mind.
The Light leads me out of the
Darkness
It gives me Hope and Courage to go on.
It is my honest and solemn prayer that
I shall always find you there.

      by the Spiritual Awareness Group of February 21, 1991

VARIATION

■ Use the process **Group Poetry** in Section II of this book to help participants create their own group message of hope.

8 GOD'S PRESENCE

Participants identify the presence or absence of God in their lives and discuss ways that they may increase their awareness of that presence.

MATERIALS

The story "Footprints."

PROCESS

1. Introduce the topic with the following comments:
   - It's comforting to feel we are in the presence of friends, family, and God.
   - During times of struggle and crisis, many people feel alone and abandoned. This feeling adds to the pain.
   - Feelings of guilt or anger often emerge as a result. This is a normal reaction.
   - In this session we'll focus on your experiences of the absence and the presence of God in your life.

2. Read all but the last paragraph of "Footprints."

   ☞ *It is likely that some participants are familiar with this story. Ask them not to discuss the conclusion.*

3. Encourage participants to reflect on the story as they consider the following questions:
   - ✔ Was there ever a particularly difficult time in your life, a time when you felt alone and sensed that God was absent?
   - ✔ What did you expect of God during that time?
   - ✔ Did you ask yourself, what did I do to deserve what is happening to me?

4. Ask those participants who are willing to briefly describe the experience they recalled.

   ☞ *Be aware of the potential for strong feelings of anger and guilt to emerge.*

5. Continue the discussion by asking some of the following questions:

©1995 Whole Person Press 210 W Michigan Duluth MN 55802   (800) 247-6789

✔ Were your expectations of God reasonable?

✔ Have your expectations changed over the years?

✔ Are your expectations of God reasonable now?

✔ What is your sense of the presence of God now?

✔ If it is different now, how is your present sense of God related to having moved through difficult experiences?

✔ What has brought you the most comfort in your life?

✔ How can you foster and nurture that which brings you comfort?

6. In closing, read "Footprints" again including the final paragraph.

VARIATION

■ Issues related to guilt and forgiveness may surface during this exercise. Consider using **Guilt and Forgiveness**, exercise 37, in this or a follow-up session.

Footprints

One night a man had a dream. He dreamed he was walking along the beach with the Lord. Across the sky flashed scenes from his life. For each scene he noticed two sets of footprints in the sand—one belonging to him and the other to the Lord.

When the last scene of his life flashed before him, he looked back at the footprints in the sand. He noticed that many times along the path of his life there was only one set of footprints. He also noticed that this happened during the lowest and saddest times in his life.

This really bothered him and he questioned the Lord about it. "Lord, you said that once I decided to follow you, you would walk with me all the way. But I noticed that during the most troublesome times in my life, there is only one set of footprints. I don't understand why, when I needed you most, you deserted me."

ᏒᎯ

The Lord replied, "My precious, precious child. I love you and I would never leave you. During your times of trial and suffering when you see only one set of footprints, it was then that I carried you."

Author unknown

©1995 Whole Person Press 210 W Michigan Duluth MN 55802   (800) 247-6789

Values

The development of values requires lifelong attention. Mature adults welcome the opportunity to reflect on their personal values and consider whether changes are in order. The exercises in this section focus on the process of developing values as well as on specific issues such as honesty and responsibility.

VALUES

9   PERSONAL VALUES I

Using discussion and a worksheet, participants identify and rank their personal values.

MATERIALS

Chalk and chalkboard; pens or pencils; **Values Ranking** worksheet.

PROCESS

1. Ask participants to reflect on the meanings they associate with the word "values."

    ☞ *Gather as many ideas from the group as you can. Listen carefully to what each person says and record it on the chalkboard. Continue for 5 minutes or until the entire board is covered with ideas.*

2. Form groups of 3 participants and ask them to write a definition of values, responding to the question: What is a personal value?

3. Reconvene the entire group and ask participants of each small group to share their definition. On the chalkboard, identify a consensus definition for the entire group.

4. Inform the group of other common characteristics and definitions of values:

    • Values are chosen freely.

    • Values are prized.

    • Values are a part of our daily lives.

    • Values guide our actions.

5. Ask the group to observe how closely their own definition fits with these other criteria.

6. Distribute the **Values Ranking** worksheet to each participant. Allow them time to review and complete the form.

7. Ask participants to share their most important and their least important value and write them on the chalkboard. Encourage participants to discuss with each other and to elaborate on the reasons for their choices of first and last ranked values.

8. In closing, encourage participants to notice how their values help them make choices as they move throughout their daily lives during the next week.

> ☞ If *Personal Values II*, *exercise 10, will be the follow-up to this session, ask participants to save their worksheets and bring them to the next meeting.*

VALUES RANKING

In the left-hand column below, a variety of values are listed. Add to the list other values that are important to you. Then in the column to the right reorder the list, according to your sense of their priorities.

Values	Importance
Money	_____
Work	_____
Love	_____
Friendship	_____
Sex	_____
Family	_____
Career	_____
Service to others	_____
Religion	_____
Leisure time	_____
Ethics	_____
Politics	_____
Social issues	_____
_____	_____
_____	_____
_____	_____
_____	_____
_____	_____
_____	_____

Note: It may be helpful to date your list and repeat this exercise each year, to track whether or not your values change over time.

10 PERSONAL VALUES II

Participants describe the factors that contribute to the formation and strengthening of values, and discover how values and beliefs affect feelings and behavior.

MATERIALS

Chalk and chalkboard; pens or pencils; **Values Reflection** worksheet.

PROCESS

☞ *If you have used* **Personal Values I**, *exercise 9, review the content and observations from that session before you begin.*

1. Introduce the subject of values and describe the purposes of this exercise:

   • To reflect on our values

   • To consider how those values were formed

   • To discuss conflicts in values

2. Distribute the **Values Reflection** worksheet and ask participants to complete it.

3. Allow participants time to share their insights with the group.

   ☞ *If the group is large, you may want to divide it into smaller discussion groups, allowing time to reconvene and discuss general insights.*

4. Ask participants to describe ways in which their values have affected their decisions and behaviors. Encourage them to be specific and give examples. Write a summary of each example on the chalkboard.

5. In closing, ask participants to identify the value or belief in their life they would most like to be remembered for at their funeral. Encourage them to share this information with each other.

VALUES REFLECTION

List three values that are most important to you and three that are of very little importance to you.

Most important to me   **Not very important to me**

_____   _____

_____   _____

_____   _____

Circle the value from the preceding list that is most important and the one that is least important to you.

Focus on the value that is most important to you as you reflect on the following questions:

1. How was this value formed? With the guidance of your parents or other mentors? From experience? Decided on your own?

   _____

   _____

2. Have your values changed over time? How? Give examples.

   _____

   _____

3. Have you ever experienced a conflict of values when you had to make a choice between two competing messages? (For instance, has addiction to alcohol or the desire to succeed in business conflicted with your love for your family?) Give examples.

   _____

   _____

4. What relationships or groups of people support your personal values and beliefs? Give examples of how each supports and strengthens your commitment to your prized values.

   _____

   _____

   _____

11 FREEDOM AND PATRIOTISM

Participants are encouraged to increase their awareness and expression of beliefs related to the concepts of freedom and patriotism.

MATERIALS

Chalk and chalkboard; paper; pens or pencils; the flag of your nation (if available).

PROCESS

1. Prior to beginning the session, set up the flag and put pencils and papers at each participant's seat.

2. Begin the group by asking each participant to identify his or her favorite patriotic song. Ask participants to describe how they feel when they hear that song sung or played.

3. Ask participants to identify a freedom or privilege they have enjoyed in their country and write it on the piece of paper. Encourage each participant to share with the group what he or she wrote and record the responses on the chalkboard.

4. After listing the responses, discuss the freedoms and privileges that were identified by the group. Ask the group for observations and comments about the list.

5. Use the **Key Experiences** process in Section II of this book to compare how this freedom or privilege was experienced in the participants' youth and how it is experienced today.

6. Ask participants to describe how their faith is associated with their sense of freedom and the commitment to their heritage and country of citizenship.

7. In closing, summarize and emphasize the common beliefs and experiences that have been expressed by the group.

12 WORK

Using discussion and a worksheet, participants define the meaning and purpose of work.

MATERIALS

Chalk and chalkboard; pens or pencils; **Jobs and Responsibilities** worksheet.

PROCESS

1. Encourage participants to define the meaning of work. (Work will be discussed as an activity of involvement both inside and outside of the home, as a volunteer, and for pay.) List the definitions on the chalkboard.

2. Distribute the worksheet and ask participants to complete it.

3. Ask participants to share their observations from the worksheet, describing their least favorite work, their most favorite work, and their insights about what they get out of work besides money for survival.

4. Lead a discussion about the observations expressed by participants. You may find the following questions to be helpful:

   ✔ When work is difficult, what can you do to make it more pleasurable or meaningful?

   ✔ If you were able to do any work you desired, can you describe the kind of work that would be? Why?

   ✔ What can you do to achieve that kind of work for yourself?

   ✔ What is the relationship between your spirituality and your attitudes, beliefs, and feelings about work?

   ✔ How does this view provide support in your working environment?

   ✔ Are there times when a hectic schedule interrupts and interferes with your sense of spirituality? When your work gets in the way of your spirituality, what changes can you make to foster and allow for spiritual peace or growth to occur?

5. In closing, summarize and emphasize common experiences and beliefs. Finally, challenge the participants to develop one idea or goal for making work a bigger part of their spiritual life.

JOBS AND RESPONSIBILITIES

Reflect on the various jobs and responsibilities you have had.

1. What was your least favorite work? Why?

_____

_____

_____

2. What was your most favorite work? Why?

_____

_____

_____

3. What satisfactions did your most favorite work give you that your
   most disliked job did not? (List at least five items.)

- _____

- _____

- _____

- _____

- _____

- _____

- _____

Comments

4. What do you want to get out of work besides money for survival?
   (List at least five elements.)

- _____

- _____

- _____

- _____

- _____

- _____

- _____

Comments

©1995 Whole Person Press 210 W Michigan Duluth MN 55802   (800) 247-6789

13 MONEY

Participants define and describe the value of money in their lives and the relationship between their view of money and their spirituality.

MATERIALS

Chalk and chalkboard; pens or pencils; **Money** worksheet.

PROCESS

1. Encourage participants to describe what money can and cannot do for them. Record the highlights of the group's comments on the chalkboard in two separate columns.

2. Distribute the **Money** worksheet and ask participants to complete it.

3. Ask participants to share their insights. The following questions might be used to elicit discussion:

   ✔ What are the problems people have with money?

   ✔ How do finances affect relationships?

   ✔ Why is money such a difficult subject in our society?

   ✔ Are there any conflicts between your beliefs about money and your spiritual beliefs?

   ✔ In what ways is money a tool that helps you put your spiritual beliefs into action?

   ✔ If you could change a current practice or view regarding money, what would that be?

4. In closing, challenge each participant to develop one idea or goal for making money a larger part of their spiritual life. Ask them to write it at the bottom of the worksheet. If time allows, encourage participants to share their goal.

©1995 Whole Person Press 210 W Michigan Duluth MN 55802   (800) 247-6789

58   Working with Groups on Spiritual Themes

MONEY

Define wealth: _____

_____

Define poverty: _____

_____

What is the relationship between happiness and money? Can a
person be both poor and happy? Rich and unhappy? Why? Give
examples from your own life.

_____

_____

_____

How did you get your attitudes and beliefs about money? From whom?

_____

_____

What were you taught about money? What messages and phrases?

_____

_____

How have your ideas about money changed?

_____

_____

(Complete this sentence at the end of the session)

> To make money a part of my expression of spiritual values, I would
>
> like to: _____
>
> _____
>
> _____
>
> _____

©1995 Whole Person Press 210 W Michigan Duluth MN 55802   (800) 247-6789

14 HONESTY

Participants explore the meaning of honesty and its value and discuss how they can maintain integrity.

MATERIALS

Pens or pencils; paper.

PROCESS

1. Discuss the meaning of honesty with participants. Ask them to share an experience from their childhood when they told a lie. Encourage them to share how they felt by asking the following questions:

   ✔ Were you caught in your lie?

   ✔ Did you swear to never tell another lie again?

   ✔ How did you feel about yourself after you told the lie?

   ✔ How did you feel toward the person you lied to?

2. Ask the participants to write, in paragraph form, their responses to the following questions:

   ✔ What is your personal belief about the value and importance of honesty?

   ✔ Must you always be honest? When is it important to be completely honest? Are there circumstances when it is better to lie?

   ✔ Is it ever OK to tell a white lie? Why? Why not?

3. Encourage participants to share their answers with each other and to discuss the responses of the group.

4. In addition, you may want to stimulate discussion with some of the following questions:

   ✔ How do you define honesty?

   ✔ How highly do you value honesty?

   ✔ What factors do you associate with honesty?

   ✔ How was your view of honesty developed?

   ✔ How is our view of honesty associated with our spirituality?

©1995 Whole Person Press 210 W Michigan Duluth MN 55802   (800) 247-6789

✔ How does one cope with dishonesty?

✔ Is it more difficult to be honest with yourself or others? Please give examples.

✔ How do we maintain the strength and integrity of our own honesty?

5. Ask participants if they have ever tried to teach a younger person about honesty. Encourage them to share examples of their experiences.

6. In closing, summarize the positive aspects of the discussion as well as the insights and opinions that have been expressed.

VARIATION

■ Use the **Word Flower** or **Word Wisdom** process in Section II of this book to add creativity to this exercise.

15 RESPONSIBILITIES

Participants discuss responsibilities, the changes that occur in life, and the adaptations that can be made.

MATERIALS

Chalk and chalkboard; dictionary.

PROCESS

1. Ask participants the following questions and record the highlights of the discussion on the chalkboard:

    ✔ How do you define responsibilities? Obligations?

    ✔ What is the difference between the two? (Encourage participants to give specific examples.)

    ✔ How do your values relate to your sense of responsibility?

    ✔ How does your sense of responsibility change depending on your role:

    As a spouse?

    As a parent?

    As a worker?

    ✔ How does your sense of responsibility change depending on where you are and your state of well being:

    At home?

    At church?

    In retirement?

    In disability?

    ✔ How have your views on responsibility changed over the years? (Encourage participants to share specific examples.)

    ✔ How are responsibility and spirituality related?

    ✔ How do you feel when you have not followed through on a responsibility or an obligation? What changes would you like to make in regard to your responsibilities and your sense of fulfilling them?

2. In closing, encourage participants to rely on their individual sense of spirituality, and summarize and emphasize the connection of one's

value association and sense of responsibility. Encourage people to take responsibility for making the decisions they need to make based on their values and beliefs about what is most important. Emphasize the power that individuals have to take control of their lives.

Creativity and Wonder

In the process of becoming adults, many people become
excessively self-critical. They lose a childlike sense of
wonder and the courage to be creative. The exercises in
this section connect creativity and wisdom with spirituality.
They encourage people to value what they have already
learned and to try new activities.

CREATIVITY AND WONDER

16 SENSES

Through group discussion and the use of props to evoke expression, participants increase their awareness of the connection between the senses and appreciation for the world, relationships, and spirituality.

MATERIALS

Chalk and chalkboard; the poem "It Has Been a Long, Cold Winter" or other poems; props, such as fabrics, scents, and candy.

PROCESS

☞ *Prior to the session, select props that stimulate each of the senses and arrange them on a table in the center of the meeting room.*

1. Begin the exercise by asking participants the following questions and writing their responses on the chalkboard:

   ✔ Do we express our spirituality through our senses?

   ✔ What senses are used to express and to appreciate spirituality?

2. Ask participants to describe several ways that feelings such as love, caring, compassion, or appreciation may be initiated in the senses. In what ways do senses stimulate feelings? For example: ·

   ✔ When you hear a cry for help, do you feel compassion?

   ✔ When you see a newborn child, do you feel nurturing?

3. Ask the participants to describe several ways that these feelings can be expressed through the senses. In what ways do senses help us express feelings? For example:

   ✔ When you smell the aroma of flowers, do you feel sad or are your feelings pleasant?

   ✔ When you see a crucifix, do you respond with faith?

   ✔ When you feel a pat on the back, do you feel reassured?

4. Pass around several props among the participants. Encourage each person to hold, smell, touch, or taste the prop as appropriate and notice their sensations. Ask them to give a one or two word description of their thoughts or feelings when experiencing each prop. Record their responses on the chalkboard.

©1995 Whole Person Press 210 W Michigan Duluth MN 55802   (800) 247-6789

5. After all the props have been experienced, discuss the responses each participant made. Group the responses into categories and identify spiritual themes, if possible.

6. In closing, read the poem "It Has Been a Long, Cold Winter," or your own favorite poem about sense, feelings, and awakenings. With the permission of the participants, ask them to hold hands and to observe a quiet moment of reflection. After a period of silence, encourage comments on the experience of touch. Express appreciation for the contributions of the participants.

☞ *Props are particularly helpful when working with the cognitively impaired. However, discussions about ways to appreciate our world and relationships in light of our spirituality can be of value to people of all ages and abilities.*

It Has Been a Long, Cold Winter

It has been a long, cold winter and I have been snuggled
in my thick blankets behind a closed, locked door;
Nestled securely with my dreams while I gently rest
in slumber, and afraid to walk across the floor;
But I can sleep no more!
My eyes open and I boldly run outside into the warm,
awaiting arms of the wonderful sunshine;
The freshness of the day is so exhilarating—all my senses
enhanced and I'm feeling alive and fine;
It's time to live my life as if it were mine!

by Richard Reed Root

17 WONDER AND MIRACLES

Using poetry and discussion, participants reflect on and develop awareness of the positive and special aspects of life.

MATERIALS

Chalk and chalkboard; pens or pencils; pictures that inspire wonder (for example, pictures of nature or of children); masking tape; **Wonder and Miracles** worksheet; the poem "The Sun Shines Upon the Water."

PROCESS

☞ *Prior to the session, tape the pictures you have selected on the walls of the meeting room.*

1. To set the tone and introduce the exercise, read a selected poem about wonder and miracles. Use one of your favorites or "The Sun Shines Upon the Water" and distribute the **Wonder and Miracles** worksheet.

2. Lead the group through a discussion and ask the following questions, recording the highlights on the chalkboard:

   ✔ When you were young, what are some things that you thought were amazing or full of wonder?

   ✔ As you have grown older, what do you now view with wonder or see as miraculous?

3. Ask participants to complete the **Wonder and Miracles** worksheet.

4. Encourage participants to share their insights with the group.

5. As time allows, stimulate discussion by asking the following questions:

   ✔ Are miracles real or imagined?

   ✔ Do miracles defy natural law?

   ✔ What is the source of a miracle?

   ✔ In what ways are miracles related to your spiritual beliefs?

   ✔ Are there ways we can increase our awareness of wonder and miracles in our lives?

6. In closing, summarize the contributions of each participant and close with a statement about the importance of wonder and miracles in our lives.

The Sun Shines Upon the Water

The sun shines upon the water as its reflections
dance with romantic enthusiasm against the
shore . . .
Just like the eyes of a princess whom I will
always adore;
Warm, soothing rays penetrate my skin while the
cool, gentle air embraces my soul with a
divine
tranquility and I can't help but stare;
Captured by the majesty of the moment adorned
with a radiating dignity touches me so very
deep;
Filled with a sense of magnificent royalty watching
the ocean splash with such loyalty is a
feeling I long
to keep;
Surrounded by a beautiful, unexplainable intelligence
displays a wonderful, enchanting elegance;
The smooth, magical freshness epitomizes poetry
in motion with an intense devotion.

by Richard Reed Root

WONDER AND MIRACLES

When did you ever experience a sense of wonder? Describe one

example: _____

_____

_____

_____

Describe a "miracle" experience in your life when something positive
happened that you simply could not explain. _____

_____

_____

_____

In what ways do miracles and your sense of wonder strengthen
your spiritual awareness?

- _____

- _____

- _____

- _____

18 PATHWAYS TO WISDOM

By exploring the five Pathways to Wisdom and Wonder, participants discover, experience, describe, and develop the paths that lead to appreciation, acceptance, creativity, hope, and love.

MATERIALS

Chalk and chalkboard; pens or pencils; **Pathways to Wisdom and Wonder** worksheet.

PROCESS

☞ *Prior to using this exercise, list the five Pathways to Wisdom and Wonder on the chalkboard.*

1. Introduce the five Pathways to Wisdom and Wonder listed below by making a few comments about each of them.
   - **Appreciate the present.**

     Simple pleasures sometimes go unnoticed.

     Special times with family and friends are moments to be savored.

     Awesome, wondrous experiences of life bring clarity.
   - **Accept yourself and your place in life.**

     Our strengths should be recognized and valued.

     Our limitations should be recognized and accepted.
   - **Believe that life holds new creativity and freedom.**

     Increased freedom is available as we grow older.

     The courage to explore allows us to be creative.
   - **Find hope in the face of loss.**

     Through our own pain and loss, we learn to empathize.

     Through our spiritual beliefs, we can find hope.
   - **Respond to others with love and compassion.**

     We need to love and to be loved.

     As we give love, we can also learn to receive it.

     A life of compassion for others is a life of great worth.

2. Divide the participants into five smaller groups. Assign one group to focus on each of the pathways.

3. Reconvene the group and ask participants to present their insights. You may want to stimulate discussion about each item with the following kinds of questions:

- **Appreciate the present.**
  - ✔ What does peace in your life mean?
  - ✔ How do you foster peaceful moments in your life?
  - ✔ How can you make opportunities for special times with friends and family?
  - ✔ How do you express your thanks or gratitude?
  - ✔ What are some of the awesome, wondrous experiences you have had in your life?
  - ✔ What are some of the simple pleasures that sometimes go unnoticed?
  - ✔ In what ways do your spiritual beliefs contribute to your appreciation of the present?
  - ✔ What practical goals can you set to help you develop a greater appreciation of the present?

- **Accept yourself and your place in life.**
  - ✔ How have you been affected by times of change or transition in your life, such as becoming an adult, a first job, being married or unmarried, parenting, or a major move?
  - ✔ What was helpful to you during these times?
  - ✔ What did it mean to recognize your limitations, and what did you learn from this awareness?
  - ✔ What has been most helpful to you as a result of the experience?
  - ✔ How have your spiritual beliefs helped you to accept yourself and your place in life?

- **Believe that life holds new creativity and freedom.**
  - ✔ What new interests or activities have you discovered in the last five to ten years?
  - ✔ In what ways have you found increased freedom as you have become older?
  - ✔ In what ways have your spiritual beliefs brought you a sense of freedom and contributed to your creativity?

✔ What goals could you set to increase your creativity?

For additional ideas, use questions from Creativity, exercise 20.

● **Find hope in the face of loss.**

✔ How have your spiritual beliefs given you hope?

✔ What has given you hope through difficult times?

✔ How have your spiritual beliefs helped you during times of loss and grief?

For additional ideas, use questions from Faith, exercise 3, or Coping with Loss, exercise 32.

● **Respond to others with love and compassion.**

✔ In what new ways can you love and be loved?

✔ How can you learn to feel more worthwhile?

For additional ideas, use questions from Love, exercise 27.

4. At the conclusion of the exercise, summarize the group's insights and express appreciation for their participation.

VARIATION

■ This exercise can be spread out over five separate meetings. Follow the procedure as outlined, but discuss only one pathway during each of the five sessions. Formation of small groups is optional, depending on the group size.

These five Pathways to Wisdom and Wonder are inspired by the work of Kathleen Fischer, Ph.D., Seattle University, Seattle, Washington.

PATHWAYS TO WISDOM AND WONDER

1. **Appreciate the present.** Identify a moment when you felt truly focused on the present: _____

   What did it teach you? _____

2. **Accept yourself and your place in life.** Identify an experience when you knew and accepted your limits and your place: _____

   _____

   What did it teach you? _____

3. **Believe that life holds new creativity and freedom.** When have you felt freedom or creativity that surprised you? _____

   _____

   What did that experience teach you? _____

4. **Find hope in the face of loss.** Identify an experience of personal loss: _____

   What wisdom did you learn from it? _____

5. **Respond to others with love and compassion.** When have you reached out with love and compassion?_____

   _____

   How did you feel and what did you learn? _____

   _____

   Look over your answers and record:

   Observations and insights: _____

   _____

   In which pathway do you show great strength? _____

   Which pathway offers you the most to learn at this moment? Why?

   _____

   What is your next step for increasing your wisdom and wonder?

   _____

19 FINDING MEANING IN SUFFERING

Participants identify ways one can grow spiritually and learn from painful life experiences.

MATERIALS

Chalk and chalkboard.

☞ *Before leading a group on this topic, please refer to "When Reminiscing to Too Painful" in the* **Supplementary Resources** *section of this book.*

PROCESS

1. Using the **Models and Heroes** process from Section II of this book, lead the group through the process of identifying a person whom they admire because of their growth through painful experiences and ask participants to identify the qualities of character and faith that helped that individual thrive in spite of their suffering.

2. Ask participants to share with each other the qualities they identified.

3. Stimulate further discussion with the following questions:

   ✔ When you experience or witness pain, suffering, or tragedy, what questions do you ask yourself or others? Do you ask why this has happened or why God can allow this to happen?

   ✔ In what ways do your spiritual beliefs or practices provide support, comfort, and assistance in answering these questions?

   ✔ Is it necessary to always have an answer to these questions? Why or why not?

4. Focus the discussion on identifying the meaning that can be found in suffering by using the following questions:

   ✔ Can you describe a time of pain or suffering and identify what you learned from the experience?

   ✔ Did this help you at other times in your life?

   ✔ Can you describe a time when you were able to help support or comfort someone else because you had a similar experience?

   ✔ How have you changed as a result of the suffering you have endured?

5. Summarize the individual strengths that have been discovered. You
   may wish to conclude with the chalktalk below on the meaning and
   purpose of suffering, which was developed by another spiritual awareness group, or you may encourage your group to develop their own.

   - Suffering produces growth, which enables change in behaviors,
     priorities, and philosophy.

   - Suffering clarifies our beliefs and draws our relationships closer and
     deeper.

   - Suffering develops our compassion, sensitivity, and empathy for
     others.

   - Suffering causes us to trust in God and places us in a position to
     experience God's unconditional love and forgiveness.

   - Suffering opens us to new opportunities and new purposes in our lives.

20 CREATIVITY

Participants increase their awareness of a sense of creativity, describe how their creativity relates to spirituality, and develop a desire to engage in creative activities.

MATERIALS

Chalk and chalkboard; pens or pencils; **Creativity** worksheet.

PROCESS

1. Introduce the subject of creativity by making the following points:
   - Creativity is the act of bringing something original into being.
   - Creativity may range from the simplest to the most complex forms of activity.
   - While most people don't think of themselves as creative, in reality we all create daily. The challenge is to identify our creativity.

2. Place the word "Creativity" in the center of the chalkboard (see the **Word Flower** process in Section II of this book). Ask participants to identify other words one could substitute or associate with creativity. Examples might include zest, passion, spirit, inventiveness, originality, imagination, productivity, kindness, or doing. Add their suggestions to the petals of the word flower.

3. Read the following four quotes one at a time from *The Ageless Spirit:*

   I think we are able to keep active longer provided we approach our lives with creativity. I think the mere fact that we keep doing is self creating. (Jessica Tandy, age 73, actress)

   Now I'm in the later part of my life, but I'm still learning, still learning. I learn every single day. (Mary Martin, age 74, actress)

   I really think creativity is the answer to aging, and by creativity I mean listening to one's own inner voice, to one's own ideas, to one's own aspirations. (Rollo May, age 82, therapist)

   I think that one can be creative wherever one is. You don't have to be an artist. The creative person is the person who is open to life and listening to life as it comes to him. (Beatrice Wood, age 90, ceramic artist)

4. Distribute the **Creativity** worksheet and ask participants to complete it.

5. Encourage participants to share their responses to the worksheet questions.

6. To stimulate further discussion, ask participants some of the following questions:

   ✔ What interest or activity have you developed over the last five years?

   ✔ What adjustments have you made in your creativity over your lifetime? (This refers to age-related changes and losses, and adaptations or adjustments that can be made. For example, "I used to enjoy keeping a large flower garden. I now enjoy a beautiful blooming flower on my window ledge.")

   ✔ How does creativity relate to spirituality?

   ✔ How does your spirituality help you to be a creative person?

   ✔ Have you passed on or taught a member of the younger generation a skill or creative talent?

   ✔ How do you feel when you see something you taught being demonstrated by another person?

7. Conclude this session by encouraging participants to recognize and express their creative spirit.

VARIATION

■ Depending on the amount of discussion and participation, several sessions may be needed to adequately cover this topic. Participants could be asked to bring an example of their creative work to a follow-up session.

From The ageless spirit *by Phillip L. Berman and Connie Goldman. Copyright ©1990 by Phillip L. Berman. Reprinted with permission of Ballantine Books, a Div of Random House Inc.*

CREATIVITY

What do you do that is creative?

_____

_____

What have you done in the past that was creative?

_____

_____

At what time in your life did you feel most creative?

_____

_____

What routine task could you do differently to enhance your interest or desire to do the task? For example, could you learn to sing while you do the dishes?

_____

What are the simple pleasures you enjoy in life? Hot chocolate? Cookies? Quiet time with a good book?

_____

_____

How often are you able to experience the simple pleasures in life? How could you do this more often?

_____

_____

21 WISDOM

Participants define wisdom and increase their awareness of the sources of wisdom and how wisdom can be passed on to succeeding generations.

RESOURCES

Chalk and chalkboard; pens or pencils; **Wisdom** worksheet.

PROCESS

1. Introduce the wisdom theme by using the **Word Wisdom** process in Section II of this book. Write "Wisdom is . . ." on the chalkboard and then ask participants to add endings. Record the responses on the chalkboard.

   For example: Wisdom is . . .

   - gained through experience.
   - knowledge.
   - experience and knowledge applied in living life.

2. Distribute the **Wisdom** worksheet and ask participants to complete it.

3. Lead a discussion based on their responses to the questions on the worksheet.

4. Ask each participant to identify the one facet of his or her wisdom that he or she would like to pass on to future generations as a legacy.

VARIATION

■ After the session, write down and photocopy the word expansion, and distribute it to participants as a tangible result of their accomplishments.

■ Use **Maturity and Knowledge**, exercise 34, in a follow-up session. The exercise could be divided into two sessions using the **Word Wisdom** process found in Section II of this book as a full group discussion and steps 2 through 5 as the second session.

WISDOM

In what ways are you wise?

How do people become wise?

What persons or events in your life contributed the most to your acquiring wisdom?

What is the source of your wisdom (intelligence, education, experience, God)?

In what ways do knowledge and experience relate to wisdom?

Do pain and suffering contribute to a person's wisdom?

In what ways do purpose, commitment, and persistence relate to wisdom? Do these qualities contribute to the development of a person's wisdom, or are they a result of this wisdom?

In what ways do the ability to listen, understand, and empathize relate to wisdom?

©1995 Whole Person Press 210 W Michigan Duluth MN 55802   (800) 247-6789

Relationships

We live our life in relationships—with family members, friends, and colleagues, with God, and with ourselves. These relationships bring us joy and they bring us sorrow. The exercises in this section offer the opportunity to think about and value good relationships, to begin resolving the pain of broken ones, and to consider how to develop new ones that are intimate and supportive.

RELATIONSHIPS

22 SELF-CONCEPT (p 83)

In small groups, participants review the ways in which they developed their self-concept and explore strategies for maintaining a positive self-image.

23 MEN'S ISSUES (p 85)

Through discussion and opportunities for mutual support and encouragement, participants of an all male group discuss issues of common concern.

24 WOMEN'S ISSUES (p 87)

Through discussion and opportunities for mutual support and encouragement, participants of an all female group discuss issues of common concern.

25 INTIMACY (p 89)

Participants explore issues of intimacy, including self-disclosure, getting close to another person through the sharing of thoughts and feelings, and sexuality.

26 DIVORCE (p 91)

Participants explore the meaning of the end of a relationship and discuss their beliefs about divorce.

27 LOVE (p 93)

Participants identify the meaning of love, types of love, love of self and others, and the love of God, and identify ways that they can put more love into their lives.

28 SPIRITUAL SUPPORT (p 95)

Using a checklist, participants consider the people and activities that provide spiritual support for them and consider new options for seeking spiritual support.

22 SELF-CONCEPT

In small groups, participants review the ways in which they developed their self-concept and explore strategies for maintaining a positive self-image.

MATERIALS

Chalk and chalkboard; paper; pens or pencils.

PROCESS

1. Explain the goals of the exercise:
   - To focus on how our self-image develops
   - To think about who and what contributed to our perceptions of ourself
   - To plan ways to develop and support a positive self-image

2. Ask participants to define "self-concept" and record their responses on the chalkboard.

3. Distribute paper to each participant and ask them to identify their own concept of themselves by responding to the question, "How do you see yourself?" Ask them to write three statements beginning with "I am . . . "

4. Form groups of 3–4 participants and ask them to discuss the following questions:

   ☞ *Write the questions on the chalkboard.*

   ✔ How did you develop the perceptions of yourself that are reflected in your "I am . . . " statements?

   ✔ How did you come to think of yourself as a good or bad, competent or inadequate, worthwhile or worthless person?

   ✔ What now contributes to maintaining or changing your feelings about yourself?

5. Reconvene the entire group and ask them to share the insights of their small group.

6. Summarize by making the following comments:
   - Each and every day that we live, we receive and process both positive and negative information indicating how others feel about us.

- The more negative information we receive, the more negatively we tend to feel and act.

- We have all said that we do not care what other people think about us—that we know who we are. But most of us do at times dwell on the negative things people think and say.

- Our challenge is to answer this question: How do we sort through all the positive and negative input, think about that which may be of value, keep that which is of value, and throw away that which is of no value to us?

7. Reform the small groups, post the following questions on the chalkboard, and ask the groups to discuss them:

   ✔ How can we avoid feeling inadequate and unworthy when other people express negative feelings about us?

   ✔ How can we assertively respond to inaccurate or negative feedback from others?

   ✔ How can we provide constructive, objective feedback to others?

   ✔ Is the issue of self-concept or self-esteem a spiritual issue? If so, why? If not, why?

8. Ask the groups to brainstorm ideas for helping people improve their self-concept. A recorder should list all ideas that are presented.

9. Reconvene the entire group and ask the groups to share their brainstorm ideas as you record them on the chalkboard.

10. In closing, ask each participant to select from the list on the chalkboard one technique that they will use this week to maintain a more positive self-concept.

23 MENS' ISSUES

Through discussion and opportunities for mutual support and encouragement, participants of an all male group discuss issues of common concern.

MATERIALS

Chalk and chalkboard; pens or pencils; paper.

PROCESS

1. Ask participants to list specific mens' issues that they would like to discuss. Record them on the chalkboard. You may want to include the following questions if they are not mentioned:

   ✔ How do we define and live out our roles in the home, family, church, and work force?

   ✔ How has competition affected our lives?

   ✔ In what ways do we express our feelings and sexuality differently from women?

   ✔ How can we maintain or change the image we project?

   ✔ What qualities are we most proud of?

   ✔ How do we express anger?

   ✔ What are we afraid of?

   ✔ How have we been hurt, and how have we hurt others?

   ✔ Do our actions reflect the person we believe ourselves to be?

   ✔ How can we express our spirituality?

2. Have the group select the topic they wish to discuss during this session. Taking the following questions one at a time, give participants a few minutes to note their own responses, then ask them to share their insights with the group.

   ✔ What are your beliefs or views about this issue?

   ✔ Have your views changed in the last five or ten years?

   ✔ If yes, in what way have your views changed?

   ✔ Can you describe the experience of change?

   ✔ What contributed to that change?

✔ Was it a growing experience for you?

3. In closing the session, express appreciation for the contributions of the participants. Encourage them to continue to reflect on ways they can continue to express, as men, their spirituality.

24 WOMENS' ISSUES

Through discussion and opportunities for mutual support and encouragement, participants of an all female group discuss issues of common
concern.

MATERIALS

Chalk and chalkboard; pens or pencils; paper.

PROCESS

1. Ask participants to list specific womens' issues that they would like to
   discuss. Record them on the chalkboard. You may want to include the
   following questions if they are not mentioned:

   ✔ How do we define and live out our roles in the home, family, church,
     and work force?

   ✔ How has feminism affected our lives?

   ✔ In what ways do we express our feelings and sexuality differently
     from men?

   ✔ How can we maintain or change the image we project?

   ✔ What qualities are we most proud of?

   ✔ How can we deal with the sometimes conflicting expectations of
     employers, spouses, children, parents, and friends?

   ✔ What are we afraid of?

   ✔ How have we been hurt, and how have we hurt others?

   ✔ Do our actions reflect the person we believe ourselves to be?

   ✔ How can we express our spirituality?

2. Have the group select the topic they wish to discuss during this session.
   Taking the following questions one at a time, give participants a few
   minutes to note their own responses, then ask them to share their
   insights with the group.

   ✔ What are your beliefs or views about this issue?

   ✔ Have your views changed in the last five or ten years?

   ✔ If yes, in what way have your views changed?

✔ Can you describe the experience of change?

✔ What contributed to that change?

✔ Was it a growing experience for you?

3. In closing the session, express appreciation for the contributions of the participants. Encourage them to continue to reflect on ways they can continue to express, as women, their spirituality.

25 INTIMACY

Participants explore issues of intimacy, including self-disclosure, getting close to another person through the sharing of thoughts and feelings, and sexuality.

MATERIALS

Pens or pencils; poetry that describes intimacy; pictures of lovers; **Aspects of Intimacy** worksheet.

PROCESS

☞ *Prior to beginning the session, arrange the pictures and selected readings on a table in the center of the room. Have the worksheet and writing materials available.*

1. Discuss the meaning of intimacy with the participants. Consider using one of the processes in Section II of this book to facilitate creative discussion. (Guide the group to examine the full spectrum of intimacy, not just sex.)

2. Distribute the **Aspects of Intimacy** worksheet and ask participants to complete it.

3. Using the worksheet as a guide, ask participants to reflect on the relationship they identified in question 1, sharing their responses with the group.

4. Lead a discussion using the following questions:

   ✔ In what way is intimacy related to your spirituality?

   ✔ What one thing can you do to make spirituality a significant part of your relationships?

5. In closing, summarize the contributions of participants and reinforce the importance of setting goals that will foster and enhance intimate relationships.

©1995 Whole Person Press 210 W Michigan Duluth MN 55802   (800) 247-6789

ASPECTS OF INTIMACY

1. Write the name of a person with whom you have had an intimate relationship (mother, spouse, daughter, friend, etc.):

   _____

2. Think about the person whose name you noted above. Consider whether each statement below was often, sometimes, or rarely typical of your relationship with that person. Make a check in the appropriate column.

	Often typical	Sometimes typical	Rarely typical
I could tell this person my deepest thoughts and feelings.	____	____	____
I felt comfortable being myself with this person.	____	____	____
I could allow this person to see my weaknesses.	____	____	____
I felt physically close to this person.	____	____	____
I felt spiritually close to this person.	____	____	____
I could describe this person as my soulmate.	____	____	____
Sex with this person (if a spouse or mate) was more than a physical experience.	____	____	____
How I felt for this person was similar to how this person felt about me.	____	____	____

3. List ways in which you and this person communicated intimacy.

   _____

   _____

4. How can you foster and enhance an intimate relationship?

   _____

   _____

26 DIVORCE

Participants explore the meaning of the end of a relationship and discuss their beliefs about divorce.

MATERIALS

Chalk and chalkboard; **Issues of Divorce** cards.

☞ *In most groups there will be several divorced persons, often still in significant pain. This exercise can provoke strong feelings. Be prepared and be supportive.*

PROCESS

☞ *Prepare the **Issues of Divorce** cards prior to the session by photocopying the page and cutting the cards apart.*

1. Begin the session by asking participants to define and describe the meaning of divorce in the context of their lives. Help them to broaden their concept of divorce by giving and eliciting many examples of broken relationships: parent/child, friend, business partners, etc.

2. Encourage participants to explore the issues that follow a broken relationship:

   • Explanations must be made to friends and family.

   • Feelings of hurt, guilt, and rejection must be resolved.

   • New ground rules must be created if the relationship is to continue in some other form.

   • New relationships must be established.

3. Ask participants to share their spiritual beliefs or values about divorce.

4. Ask each participant to draw an **Issues of Divorce** card. Then ask participants, in turn, to read the card and describe their views on that issue. Encourage discussion of each scenario.

5. In closing, comment on the value of each person's contribution, and express appreciation for their willingness to share painful experiences.

©1995 Whole Person Press 210 W Michigan Duluth MN 55802   (800) 247-6789

ISSUES OF DIVORCE

John and Helen have been married five years. They have no children. They decide to divorce because . . .	Ed feels guilty that he caused his divorce. Now that the relationship is over, he doesn't know how to cope. What advice could you give Ed?
John leaves Sally and their three children for another woman. This happened because . . .	Sara feels she was rejected by her husband who divorced her. She feels she will never be able to trust another man. How would you handle this situation?
Jane has just gotten divorced. How does she "celebrate" this event?	When is a divorced person ready to start a new relationship?
Mike wants to have a funeral to symbolize the "death" of his marriage. Describe some ways he might go about doing this.	Is being divorced a status symbol or a stigma?
Can persons who are divorced from each other still be friends?	Can true reconciliation occur between divorced persons?

27 LOVE

Participants identify the meaning of love, types of love, love of self and others, and the love of God, and identify ways that they can put more love into their lives.

MATERIALS

Chalk and chalkboard; pens or pencils; **Love** worksheet.

PROCESS

1. Ask participants what the word "love" means to them. Record their definitions on the chalkboard.

   ☞ *Be sure to discuss the different types of love (such as unconditional love, romantic love, sexual love, love of children or grandchildren, love of friends, and love of God).*

2. Distribute the **Love** worksheet and ask participants to complete it.

3. Encourage participants to share the insights gained from the worksheet, using some of the following questions to elicit discussion:

   ✔ What does it mean to love yourself?

   ✔ Are self-love and selfishness the same thing? Why or why not?

   ✔ Can a person really love another if he does not love himself?

   ✔ What are the beliefs that keep you from loving yourself? (Responses may be related to low self-worth and low self-image, guilt and shame, brought about by negative life experiences.)

4. Discuss the relationship between participants' spiritual beliefs and their beliefs about love.

5. Ask participants to describe a time that they have experienced unconditional love by God, by themselves, or by others.

6. Encourage participants to develop and list specific goals they can set to grow in their love of self, others, and God, and to experience the unconditional love of God. In closing, ask them to share one or more of their goals.

LOVE

Whom do I love (or have I loved in the past)? Record their names in the boxes below. In the space below each name, describe the qualities and characteristics of that loving relationship.

_____ Name	_____ Name	_____ Name

Indicate in the shaded area at the bottom of each box at which time in your life this relationship was (or will be) most loving.

Notice the similarities and differences between the three relationships and write your observations here: _____

_____

What is the relationship you have with yourself? In what ways do you (or do you not) love yourself? _____

_____

What is spiritual about love? _____

_____

Describe one time when you experienced unconditional love from God, yourself, or another person: _____

_____

Identify one change you would like to make to improve the quality of your loving relationships:_____

_____

28 SPIRITUAL SUPPORT

Using a checklist, participants consider the people and activities that provide spiritual support for them and consider new options for seeking spiritual support.

MATERIALS

Chalk and chalkboard; pens or pencils; **Sources of Spiritual Support** worksheet.

PROCESS

1. Introduce the goals of the exercise with the following comments:
   - People often need to draw on resources outside themselves for spiritual support.
   - Your spiritual life may be enriched if you look for support from many people and activities.
   - During this session, you will have the chance to share with others in your group your ways of gaining support for your spiritual beliefs.

2. Distribute the **Sources of Spiritual Support** worksheet and ask participants to complete it.

3. Reconvene the group and ask participants to list their most important sources of spiritual support, recording them on the chalkboard.

4. Ask participants whether this list triggers any additional insights.

5. Conclude by asking participants to select one new source of spiritual support and to commit themselves to exploring it during the next week.

©1995 Whole Person Press 210 W Michigan Duluth MN 55802   (800) 247-6789

SOURCES OF SPIRITUAL SUPPORT

Identify the sources from which you now receive spiritual support.
Then check the resources you would like to use in the future.

Activity	Now use	Would like to use
Worship services		
Visit with clergy		
Talk with friends		
Prayer		
Meditation		
Music		
Poetry		
Scripture		
Other books		
Rosary		
Sacraments		
Other people		
Other symbols		
Other rituals		

Place a plus sign next to the sources that are most important to you.
Place a minus sign next to those that are least important to you.

Look over your responses and write your observations, questions, and
comments about what you notice.

_____

_____

Life Review

Wise people regularly take time to reflect on their lives; only in that way can they know whether midcourse corrections are necessary. The exercises in this section facilitate that reflection by encouraging participants to consider their entire lives from birth to death. They recall the legacy they were given and consider that which they wish to pass along.

LIFE REVIEW

29 LIFE EXPERIENCES REVIEW   (p 99)

Using **Haight's Life Review and Experiencing Form**, participants review the events and feelings of each stage of their life.

30 SKILLS, TALENTS, VIRTUES   (p 104)

Participants identify their unique skills, talents, and virtues and recognize ways in which these qualities can be used to help them adapt to the events of their lives.

31 TRANSITION AND CHANGE   (p 107)

Participants explore the meaning of change and transition, and identify what can be learned from these experiences.

32 COPING WITH LOSS   (p 109)

Participants discuss the impact of loss, consider ways to positively cope with loss, and reflect on loss experiences that resulted in personal and spiritual growth.

33 HEALTHY TRAITS OF AGING   (p 112)

Participants identify the healthy traits of aging and establish goals for continued healthy growth.

34 MATURITY AND KNOWLEDGE   (p 115)

Participants identify qualities of maturity and establish goals for ongoing growth toward emotional and spiritual maturity.

35 LEGACY   (p 117)

Participants reflect on the positive aspects of the legacy they have received. They discover the legacy they hope to leave, and identify and record a goal used to establish and foster that legacy.

36 AFTERLIFE   (p 120)

Participants are encouraged to reflect on and express each person's unique beliefs about afterlife and to discover ways to utilize these beliefs beneficially during this life.

29 LIFE EXPERIENCES REVIEW

Using **Haight's Life Review and Experiencing Form**, participants review the events and feelings of each stage of their life.

MATERIALS

Chalk and chalkboard; **Haight's Life Review and Experiencing Form**.

☞ *This form should be distributed to and completed by participants prior to this session and brought to the session.*

PROCESS

1. Form groups of 3–4 participants. Ask them to discuss the observations and insights which they gained as they completed and reacted to **Haight's Life Review and Experiencing Form**. Ask each group to appoint a recorder to summarize the group's insights.

2. Reconvene the entire group and ask each reporter to summarize the small group's insights. Write a summary of each group's comments on the chalkboard.

3. Lead a group discussion regarding the immense amount of learning we collect over a lifetime and the insights which participants have gained from this life review.

   ☞ *We are pleased to provide the **Life Review and Experiencing Form** (LREF) that was developed by Barbara K. Haight, R.N., C., DrPH, Professor of Nursing at the Medical University of South Carolina, Charleston, South Carolina.*

   ***Haight's Life Review and Experiencing Form** is often used in a structured life review process which consists of eight one-hour visits, in one-to-one interviews by a professional counselor or therapist. We have adapted it here for use as a group process tool.*

   For further information you may wish to consult the following references. The use of this therapeutic intervention is described in detail in Dr. Haight's article 1989, Life review: a method for pastoral counseling, Part I. Journal of Religion and Aging, *5(3), 17–29. A concise article by Dr. Haight and Dr. Irene Burnside, which describes the application of life review and reminiscing in nursing practice is, 1992 Reminiscence and life review: Conducting the process.* Journal of Gerontological Nursing, 18*(2), 39–42. The authors differentiate between the two processes and describe the application of each.*

Dr. Haight also recommends her article 1991 Reminiscing: the state of the art as a basis for practice. International Journal of Aging and Human Development, 33*(1), 1–32, as a reference for a summary of 97 articles about reminiscing and life review.*

HAIGHT'S LIFE REVIEW AND EXPERIENCING FORM

On a sheet of paper, write short answers to the following questions.

Childhood:

1. What is the very first thing you can remember in your life? Go back as far as you can.
2. What other things can you remember about when you were very young?
3. What was life like for you as a child?
4. What were your parents like? What were their weaknesses? Their strengths?
5. Did you have any brothers or sisters? What was each one like?
6. Did someone close to you die when you were growing up?
7. Did someone important to you go away?
8. Do you ever remember being very sick?
9. Do you remember having an accident?
10. Do you remember being in a very dangerous situation?
11. Was anything important to you lost or destroyed?
12. Was church a large part of your life?
13. Did you enjoy being a boy/girl?

Adolescence:

1. When you think about yourself and your life as a teenager, what is the first thing you can remember about that time?
2. What other things stand out in your memory about being a teenager?
3. Tell me about your parents, brothers, sisters, friends, teachers, those you were especially close to, those you admired, and those you wanted to be like.
4. Did you attend church and youth groups?
5. Did you go to school? How did you feel about school?
6. Did you work during these years?
7. Tell me of any hardships you experienced at this time.
8. Do you remember feeling that there wasn't enough food or other necessities when you were a child or adolescent?
9. Do you remember feeling left alone, abandoned, not having enough love or care as a child or adolescent?
10. What were the pleasant things about your adolescence?
11. What was the most unpleasant thing about your adolescence?

©1995 Whole Person Press 210 W Michigan Duluth MN 55802   (800) 247-6789

12. All things considered, would you say you were happy or unhappy as a teenager?
13. Do you remember your first attraction to another person?
14. How did you feel about sexual activities and your own sexual identity?

Family and home:

1. How did your parents get along?
2. How did other people in your home get along?
3. What was the atmosphere in your home?
4. Were you punished as a child? For what? Who did the punishing? Who was the boss?
5. When you wanted something from your parents, how did you go about getting it?
6. What kind of a person did your parents like the most? The least?
7. Who were you closest to in your family?
8. Who in your family were you most like? In what way?
9. What place did religion play in your family life?

Adulthood:

1. What are the most important events that happened in your adulthood?
2. What was life like for you in your twenties and thirties?
3. What kind of person were you? What did you enjoy?
4. Tell me about your work. Did you enjoy your work? Did you earn an adequate living? Did you work hard during those years? Were you appreciated?
5. Did you form significant relationships with other people?
6. If you married, what kind of person was your spouse?
7. If you did not marry, why not?
8. Do you think marriages get better or worse over time? Were you married more than once?
9. On the whole, would you say you had a happy or unhappy marriage?
10. Was sexual intimacy important to you?
11. What were some of the main difficulties you encountered during your adult years?
    a. Did someone close to you die? Go away?
    b. Were you ever sick? Have an accident?
    c. Did you move often? Change jobs?
    d. Did you ever feel alone? Abandoned?
    e. Did you ever feel needy?

©1995 Whole Person Press 210 W Michigan Duluth MN 55802   (800) 247-6789

Summary:

1. On the whole, what kind of life do you think you've had?
2. If everything were to be the same, would you like to live your life over again?
3. If you were going to live your life over again, what would you change? Leave unchanged?
4. Consider your overall feelings and ideas about your life. What would you say the three main satisfactions in your life have been? Why were they satisfying?
5. Everyone has had disappointments. What have been the main disappointments in your life?
6. What was the hardest thing you had to face in your life? Please describe it.
7. What was the happiest period of your life? What made it the happiest period? Why is your life less happy now?
8. What was the saddest period of your life? Why is your life happier now?
9. What was the proudest moment in your life?
10. If you could stay the same age all your life, what age would you choose? Why?
11. How do you think your life has worked out? Better or worse than what you had hoped for?
12. What are the best things about the age you are now?
13. What are the worst things about the age you are now?
14. What are the most important things to you in your life today?
15. What do you hope will happen to you as you grow older?
16. What do you fear will happen to you as you grow older?
17. What are your reactions to this review of your life?

Gorney, J. 1968. Experiencing and age: Patterns of reminiscence among the elderly. Ph.D. diss., University of Chicago.

Falk, J. 1969. The organization of remembered life experience of older people: Its relation to anticipated stress, to subsequent adaptation and to age. Ph.D. diss., University of Chicago.

30 SKILLS, TALENTS, VIRTUES

Participants identify their unique skills, talents, and virtues and recognize ways in which these qualities can be used to help them adapt to the events of their lives.

MATERIALS

Chalk and chalkboard; pens or pencils; a dictionary; **Skills, Talents, and Virtues** worksheet.

PROCESS

1. Announce to the group that the purpose of this session is to discover how to adapt past skills to provide coping strength in the present.

2. Using a dictionary as a guide, discuss the various meanings of the words skill, talent, and virtue. Discuss the similarities. Record key elements of the definitions on the chalkboard.

3. Distribute the worksheet and have participants complete question 1. Encourage the group to reflect on and to identify the skills, talents, and virtues they developed in earlier stages of their lives (childhood, adolescence, young adulthood, middle years, and later years).

4. Lead a discussion built on participant's worksheet notes. Record responses on the chalkboard. Continue by asking the following questions:

   ✔ How do we acquire skills, talents, and virtues?

   ✔ Has anyone ever used a skill to help you? In what way?

   ✔ Have you used a skill or talent to help others? How?

5. Tell participants to place an asterisk by any skills, talents, or virtues that they believe they have lost or forgotten. Ask the following questions:

   ✔ Are skills or talents really lost? Why?

   ✔ Can they be redeveloped? How?

6. Provide the following information: Sometimes a skill or talent we once had needs to be adapted to accommodate for change or loss. For instance, a master gardener may lose mobility but still enjoy planting container gardens.

7. Ask participants to complete question 2 of the worksheet as they consider how they can retain and regain skills, talents, and virtues that might otherwise be lost. Discuss the following questions:

✔ What adaptations have you made?

✔ What adaptations can you make?

8. Discuss with the group the relationship between a person's spirituality and his or her skills, talents, and virtues. Discuss what aspects of spirituality can help the person to adapt to changes or losses.

9. Ask participants to set specific goals by using question 3 of the worksheet and sharing their responses with each other as a closing.

VARIATION

■ Use **Legacy**, exercise 35, as a follow-up to this session.

SKILLS, TALENTS, AND VIRTUES

1. List the skills, talents, and virtues you have or once had.

    Skills: _____

    _____

    _____

    Talents: _____

    _____

    _____

    Virtues: _____

    _____

    _____

2. List adaptations that can help you maintain your skills and talents.

    Adaptations I have made: _____

    _____

    _____

    Adaptations I can make: _____

    _____

    _____

3. List ways in which you will cultivate your skills, talents, and virtues

    in the present and the future: _____

    _____

    _____

    _____

    _____

31 TRANSITION AND CHANGE

Participants explore the meaning of change and transition, and identify what can be learned from these experiences.

MATERIALS

Chalk and chalkboard; pens or pencils; **Change** worksheet.

PROCESS

1. Ask participants to define the word transition. (Use one of the processes in Section II of this book to stimulate the group's thinking.) Be sure to discuss the variety of transitions one makes during a lifetime. Some examples are starting school, finishing school, job changes, marriage, childbirth, health changes, children leaving home, and retirement.

2. Distribute the worksheet and ask participants to identify an important change in their lives and the impact it had on them. Ask them to complete all but the final worksheet question.

3. Ask participants to share something about the change they identified and the factors involved in that change. List the changes in a column on the left side of the chalkboard.

4. Explain that change can be difficult and that rituals can help us accept change and move on. Encourage the group to dream up ceremonies to help with transitions. Begin by asking participants if any type of ceremony or ritual helped them deal with the reality of a change that is listed on the chalkboard. Record the ritual to the right of the appropriate change. Continue by asking them to create rituals that could be used for the changes that didn't seem to have a ritual.

5. Conclude by asking people to identify on their worksheets one idea they would like to remember from this session. Encourage them to share that insight with the group.

©1995 Whole Person Press 210 W Michigan Duluth MN 55802   (800) 247-6789

CHANGE

Identify a very important change or transition in your life (the first one that comes to your mind is fine). _____

_____

Describe the impact of that change on you and your life.

_____

_____

Answer the following questions about the change:

Was it planned or unplanned? _____

What were the positive effects? _____

_____

What were the negative effects? _____

_____

How much control over the experience did you have? _____

_____

What lessons did you learn from the experience? How can this help in the present? _____

How did you deal with it? _____

How else could you have dealt with it? _____

Was a ceremony involved to signal the change (wedding, baptism, graduation)? _____

What other means have been helpful in the coping process (family, friends, church, prayer, work)? _____

Observations: _____

_____

What insight do you want to remember from this session? (Complete this question at the end of this session.) _____

_____

32 COPING WITH LOSS

Participants discuss the impact of loss, consider ways to positively cope with loss, and reflect on loss experiences that resulted in personal and spiritual growth.

MATERIALS

Chalk and chalkboard, pens or pencils; **Losses** worksheet.

PROCESS

☞ *Loss always produces grief. This session will require you to give people ample time to think, to share their experiences, and to express their feelings. If someone appears to be in crisis, you may want to arrange for individual counseling or recommend a grief support group.*

1. Explain to the group that the goal of this session not only is to identify losses, but to learn to view losses as providing an opportunity for personal and spiritual growth.

2. Introduce the topic of loss, by making the following points, encouraging the group to discuss each item:

    • To suffer a loss is not only to lose possession of something but also to be separated from someone.

    • Dealing with loss is one of the major spiritual challenges.

    • Losses occur throughout our lives, but they often come at a faster pace in the later years.

    • Successful aging calls for a revision of values; it is a chance to discover new sources of self-worth.

    • How we deal with the experience of loss is one of the most critical factors in our sense of happiness or unhappiness.

3. Distribute the **Losses** worksheet and ask participants to complete it.

4. Use the following questions to encourage discussion of the worksheet:

    ✔ What has been most helpful to you during a time of loss?

    ✔ Can you identify a loss that contributed to your personal or spiritual growth—that brought you to a new understanding?

5. Post the following list on the chalkboard and point to each item as you ask people to focus on activities that both prepare them for loss, help them heal from it, and learn the most from it.

- Improved communication with friends and family
- Time to enjoy people and activities
- Time to help and listen
- Hobbies and new activities
- The opportunity to truly be yourself
- A change in values from material to spiritual
- The nourishment of new hopes
- The opportunity to learn new things
- The ability to laugh at life—transforming dismay into humor
- Learning to live with circumstances we cannot change

6. Form groups of 3–4 participants. Ask participants to brainstorm ideas that will help individuals prepare for a loss. One person should act as a recorder.

7. Reconvene the group. In closing, ask each small group to share the insights of its participants with the entire group. Encourage them to begin using some of the ideas that are mentioned to prepare for inevitable losses.

©1995 Whole Person Press 210 W Michigan Duluth MN 55802 (800) 247-6789

LOSSES

Identify losses that you have experienced. These may include the loss of loved ones, a home or career, physical or mental health, or any other important person, possession, or faculty.

Losses that you
have experienced

Learning and growth
related to that loss

_____   _____

_____   _____

_____   _____

_____   _____

In the list below, check activities that have helped you deal with loss and feel free to add your own at the bottom of the list.

_____   Acknowledging thoughts and feelings

_____   Talking

_____   Quiet time

_____   Prayer, meditation

_____   Worship

_____   Creative expression—poetry, journaling

_____   Symbolic ceremonies

_____   Reading

_____   Acts of kindness

_____   Time with family or friends

_____   Visits with clergy

_____   Volunteering

_____   Forgiveness of self, others, and God

_____

_____

33 HEALTHY TRAITS OF AGING

Participants identify the healthy traits of aging and establish goals for continued healthy growth.

MATERIALS

Chalk and chalkboard; paper; pens or pencils; **Healthy Traits of Aging** worksheet.

PROCESS

1. As a warm-up, read the following paragraph written by a real expert on aging, Beatrice Wood, age 90, a ceramic artist:

   There is no question that the outside of an individual does change and wither and wrinkle, but curiously the inside does not change, and you will hear ever so many people say that. Even if they are old crocks, they will say, I don't feel old. Age is very mysterious because the essence of the human being— the soul—actually never ages. It's only the outer covering of the individual that changes.

2. Using the **Models and Heroes** process in Section II of this book, ask participants to identify someone they know who is growing old gracefully.

3. Ask participants to share what they have written and record their responses on the chalkboard.

4. Distribute the worksheet and ask participants to complete it.

5. Lead a discussion of the insights participants have written on their worksheets. You might want to supplement this discussion by using the following questions:

   ✔ Which of the positive qualities of aging do you exhibit? (Encourage each participant to claim at least one positive quality even if they are still young.)

   ✔ What is perseverance? Persistence? Discipline? Patience?

   ✔ How do these qualities relate to you?

   ✔ What traits do you notice when a person is not growing old gracefully? Do you have any of these traits?

©1995 Whole Person Press 210 W Michigan Duluth MN 55802   (800) 247-6789

✔ When you look at the positive qualities listed, where do you think people get the strength, wisdom, or grace to live out that quality?

✔ In what way does your sense of spirituality relate to these positive qualities?

✔ How do you nurture, foster, and get in touch with the positive qualities in yourself?

✔ What goals might you set to experience graceful aging?

6. Conclude the session by summarizing the contributions of the participants and providing positive reinforcement and encouragement for the goals they have established.

HEALTHY TRAITS OF AGING
(How to grow older with grace and dignity)

List characteristics of people who are aging gracefully: _____

_____

_____

On what sources of strength, wisdom, and grace can we draw as we age? _____

_____

_____

How can we nurture and foster these strengths? _____

_____

_____

In what ways can we become more spiritual as we age? _____

_____

_____

Because I want to grow older with grace and dignity:

I will _____

I will _____

I will _____

I will _____

I will _____

I will _____

34 MATURITY AND KNOWLEDGE

Participants identify qualities of maturity and establish goals for ongoing growth toward emotional and spiritual maturity.

MATERIALS

Chalk and chalkboard; paper; pens or pencils; the poem, "Maturity."

PROCESS

1. As an introduction to the theme, read the poem "Maturity" that is printed at the end of this exercise.

2. Encourage participants to briefly share their definition of wisdom and knowledge. Ask participants to describe the gap that may exist between knowledge and the application of knowledge.

3. Use the **Word Wisdom** process in Section II of this book to expand the concepts of maturity, wisdom, and knowledge.

4. Ask participants to personalize the concept of maturity by answering the following questions, first on paper and then in discussion. Record highlights on the chalkboard.

   ✔ What is one quality of maturity that you possess?

   ✔ Is maturity related to age?

   ✔ In what ways do knowledge, experience, and wisdom relate to maturity?

   ✔ What are the qualities you associate with a mature person?

   ✔ Can you describe a person who exhibits these qualities? In what ways does he or she exhibit these qualities?

   ✔ In what ways does responsibility relate to maturity?

   ✔ How does living through a difficult or painful experience relate to maturity? Have you experienced such a time? In what ways did you mature as a result of this experience?

   ✔ Is there such a thing as spiritual maturity? What are the qualities of spiritual maturity? Are you spiritually mature? What experiences contribute to the development of that maturity?

5. Help participants set goals to foster the development of emotional and spiritual maturity. Ask them to write these goals on paper, then to share them with the group.

VARIATION

■ At the conclusion of this session you may wish to help your group write a poem that reflects what they have discussed. Use the **Group Poetry** process in Section II of this book to assist you. If you write the poem on paper, photocopy it and distribute a copy to participants. It will serve as a record of their discussion.

Maturity

Maturity is acknowledging we can
continue to learn and grow
throughout life
Maturity is not age related
Maturity is being accountable
and accepting responsibility
Maturity is finding the
opportunity in a problem
Maturity is persistence
Maturity is supporting
prized values and beliefs
Maturity is respect for others
Maturity is reaching out a
helping hand
Maturity is wisdom well
used
(Wisdom is experience, knowledge
and
spirituality)
Maturity is a forgiving heart
Maturity is using God's gifts
well . . .

by the Spiritual Awareness Group of August 5, 1992

35 LEGACY

Participants reflect on the positive aspects of the legacy they have received. They discover the legacy they hope to leave, and identify and record a goal used to establish and foster that legacy.

MATERIALS

Chalk and chalkboard; pens or pencils; physical symbols of legacy—an old Bible, a poetry book with inscriptions, an item of jewelry; **Legacy** worksheet; the poem, "Kind Deeds."

PROCESS

☞ *Prior to the group session, arrange the props—the Bible, poetry book, and jewelry—on a table in the center of the room.*

1. Introduce the concept of legacy by making the following points:

   - A legacy is something tangible or intangible handed down from the past.

   - Although a legacy may have both positive and negative character-istics, the focus of our discussion is on positive values.

2. Draw attention to the objects you have collected and pass them around to the participants. Encourage them to reflect and comment on the thoughts, memories, or feelings that may be evoked by these objects.

3. Lead participants through the worksheet section by section, pausing after each section has been completed to discuss their insights.

4. Summarize the contributions of participants and encourage them to reflect on a legacy they hope to leave and to start steps toward that goal.

5. In closing, ask a participant to read the poem "Kind Deeds."

VARIATION

■ At the previous group meeting, ask participants to bring to this session 2 or 3 items that are important to them and that demonstrate a portion of their legacy. Encourage them to show their items and discuss their meaning. This process will make the session richer and more personal.

Kind Deeds

Bless you my dears
You're worth your weight in gold
The good you do for others
Will never be fully told
But the roots of life run deeply
And its branches tower high
Good seeds, sown freely here
Will blossom in the sky

by Dovie Lee Manning

©1995 Whole Person Press 210 W Michigan Duluth MN 55802   (800) 247-6789

LEGACY

Reflect on the tangible and intangible aspects of the legacy you have received and that which you want to pass on. Fill in the space with words and phrases rather than complete sentences.

Identify legacies from your past:

Comment on the positive and negative aspects of those legacies:

List the legacies you would like to leave for future generations:

List the steps you will take to ensure that your legacy will actually be carried out:

36 AFTERLIFE

Participants are encouraged to reflect on and express each person's unique beliefs about afterlife and to discover ways to utilize these beliefs beneficially during this life.

MATERIALS

Chalk and chalkboard; paper; pens or pencils.

PROCESS

1. Introduce the exercise as a discussion about beliefs and concepts concerning the meaning of life, death, and afterlife.

2. Distribute a blank sheet of paper to each participant.

3. Ask the following questions one at a time, encouraging people to write their answer on the paper. Hold a short discussion, allowing everyone to contribute and record the comments on the chalkboard before proceeding to the next question.

   ✔ If this were your last day on earth, how would you want to spend your time?

   ✔ What do you think happens at the moment of death?

   ✔ What is your image of the afterlife? Turn your paper over and take a few minutes to draw a picture of it.

   ✔ Do you believe in the concept of heaven? If so, what will heaven be like for you?

   ✔ Do you believe in the concept of hell? If so, what do you believe hell is like and why will some people experience it?

   ✔ How do your beliefs about the afterlife influence you today? Share an example.

4. Close the group by challenging each participant to pick one thing that they really want to do and do it today, instead of waiting until the end of their life.

©1995 Whole Person Press 210 W Michigan Duluth MN 55802   (800) 247-6789

Ceremonies

Ceremonies mark milestones in our lives. A wedding means that we are married—no doubt about it. Because ceremonies are so powerful, they can be developed to celebrate, to commemorate, and to bring closure for any major life experience. The exercises in this brief section, explore the healing nature of symbols, rituals, and ceremonies.

CEREMONIES

37 GUILT AND FORGIVENESS   (p 123)

Using discussion, handouts, and a ceremony, participants are encouraged to identify ways to let go of guilt and experience forgiveness.

38 PRAYER AND MEDITATION   (p 126)

Participants are encouraged to increase their awareness of prayer, meditation, and worship and to explore the function of each in their personal spiritual lives.

39 SYMBOLS AND RITUALS   (p 128)

Through discussion and participation in a symbolic ceremony, participants identify how one can express emotion through the use of symbols and rituals.

37 GUILT AND FORGIVENESS

Using discussion, handouts, and a ceremony, participants are encouraged to identify ways to let go of guilt and experience forgiveness.

MATERIALS

Waste basket; paper; pens or pencils; chalk and chalkboard; **Guilt and Forgiveness** worksheet.

☞ *Forgiveness is one of the most frequently discussed issues in a spiritual awareness group. The first half of this exercises deals with guilt; the second half focuses on the means of forgiveness and offers a surrender ceremony.*

PROCESS

1. Introduce the subject of guilt and forgiveness by discussing the word "guilt" and by reading and discussing point-by-point, the "Steps to Forgiveness" list which is at the end of this exercise.

2. Distribute the worksheet and ask participants to complete Part I.

3. Discuss participants' reactions to the worksheet questions, stimulating discussion with the following questions as needed:

   ✔ Are there any positive aspects of feeling guilty?

   ✔ Is all guilt unhealthy?

   ✔ Do you need to be perfect to feel guilt free?

   ✔ How does your view of God relate to your feelings of guilt and the resolution of those feelings?

4. Ask participants to complete Part II of the worksheet.

5. Encourage participants to share their observations, stimulating the discussion by using some of the following questions:

   ✔ What is forgiveness?

   ✔ How do feelings of anger, bitterness, and resentment relate to forgiveness?

   ✔ How are we forgiven? How do we receive forgiveness from ourselves, from others, and from God?

✔ Can you describe a time when you forgave yourself, another person, or God?

✔ In which area is forgiveness easiest?

✔ What is your response to the "Steps to Forgiveness" list?

✔ Can you describe the freedom of forgiveness?

6. Lead participants through the surrender ceremony—a symbolic activity to assist them in letting go of guilt and accepting forgiveness. Place a waste basket in the center of the room; distribute paper and pencils to each participant; and provide the following instructions:

➤ Take a few minutes to reflect on a source of guilt for you.

➤ In a symbolic way, record this source of guilt on the piece of paper.

➤ Crumple the paper into a ball, and as you place the paper in the trash can, also discard the guilt.

7. Conclude the session by asking participants to complete and discuss Part III of the worksheet. Express appreciation for the group's willingness to face the often painful issue of guilt and forgiveness.

Steps to Forgiveness

Acknowledge and identify the real problem.
Accept your responsibility. Ask, What was my responsibility?
Ask yourself, Do I really want to be forgiven or do I want to continue to suffer?
Forgive others involved.
Forgive yourself.

Reprinted from Healing for damaged emotions *by D. Seamands, published by Victor Books, (1981), SP Publications, Inc., Wheaton, IL 60187.*

©1995 Whole Person Press 210 W Michigan Duluth MN 55802   (800) 247-6789

GUILT AND FORGIVENESS

Part I: Guilt

Make a note of something about which you are feeling guilty:

_____

What is causing your feeling of guilt? _____

_____

What does your guilt feel like? _____

_____

What is guilt? (Define it in light of your experience.) _____

_____

Part II: Forgiveness

Identify an experience when you felt forgiven: _____

_____

How did the forgiveness happen? (Did God forgive you, someone
else forgive you, or did you forgive yourself?)_____

_____

How did the forgiveness feel to you? _____

_____

Identify a time when you forgave someone else: _____

_____

Did they have to apologize or make recompense before you
allowed yourself to forgive them? _____

_____

How did it feel to forgive someone? _____

Part III: Key insights you want to remember from this session:

_____

_____

_____

38 PRAYER AND MEDITATION

Participants are encouraged to increase their awareness of prayer, meditation, and worship and to explore the function of each in their personal spiritual lives.

MATERIALS

Chalk and chalkboard; poems about prayer; a picture or figurine of the Praying Hands; recorded hymns; recorded nature sounds.

PROCESS

☞ *Prior to beginning the session, set up the picture or figurine of the Praying Hands. Be sure that this session is conducted in a peaceful environment. Soft inspirational music and subdued lighting will set a meditative mood. A lighted candle could be placed on a table in the center of the room.*

1. Gently introduce the theme with an opening visualization or meditation followed by a few minutes of quiet. This process, **Quieting Visualization**, is described in Section II of this book.

2. Ask participants to reflect on this experience, describing to each other some of their thoughts and feelings.

3. Ask participants the following question: Was this experience for you one of meditation? Of prayer? Of worship? Why or why not?

4. Ask participants to define prayer, meditation, and worship. Record their responses on the chalkboard.

   ☞ *Help the group create its own definition. Be sure to encourage attitudes of listening and acceptance rather than argument. Each viewpoint should be considered to be true for the person who expresses it.*

5. Continue the discussion by asking some of the following questions:

   ✔ What are some ways in which people pray, meditate, and worship?

   ✔ In what ways are prayer, meditation, and worship alike? In what ways are they different?

   ✔ When do you pray, meditate, or worship?

✔ Where do you pray, meditate, or worship?

✔ How does commitment relate to prayer, meditation, and worship?

✔ What indications have you received of an answer to prayer?

✔ When is it most difficult for you to pray?

✔ Was there a time in your life when prayer was most important? What was your experience?

✔ The saying goes "Prayer changes things." Have you experienced this to be true? What was your experience?

✔ In what ways are prayer and meditation linked to our spiritual experience?

6. With the permission and agreement of all participants, conclude the session with prayer.

39 SYMBOLS AND RITUALS

Through discussion and participation in a symbolic ceremony, participants identify how one can express emotion through the use of symbols
and rituals.

MATERIALS

A variety of symbolic items including a candle plus other items such as
flowers, a cross, and a Star of David; chalk and chalkboard; pens or pencils;
Symbols and Rituals worksheet.

PROCESS

☞ *Prior to the session, arrange the symbolic items on a table in the
center of the room.*

1. Begin by explaining to participants that the purpose of the discussion
   is to examine the use of symbols and rituals as a form of expression in
   celebration, commemoration, and worship.

2. Explain that there will be a demonstration of symbolic expression.
   Light the candle at this time.

3. Ask participants what a lighted candle represents to them and record
   their observations on the chalkboard.

4. Distribute the worksheet and have participants complete Part I. Encourage them to identify specific symbols or rituals associated with their
   culture or spiritual affiliation that have significant meaning to them.
   Ask them to describe the feelings, thoughts, and responses associated
   with the symbol or ritual.

5. Lead a discussion, asking participants to share their list of symbols and
   rituals and describe their meaning. In addition, to stimulate discussion,
   you may wish to focus on the other worksheet questions or the
   following possibilities:

   ✔ What are other symbolic ways you have used ritual and tradition?

   ✔ How can you enhance the awareness of your feelings through the use
     of symbolic or ceremonial expression?

✔ How can you enhance your sense of peace and worship through further use of symbolic or ceremonial expression?

6. Encourage participants to record on the worksheet their thoughts, observations, and insights on this session.

7. In closing, summarize and emphasize the goals of enhanced expression. For a short closing ceremony, consider asking the participants to hold hands in a circle and repeat the lighted candle statements.

VARIATION

■ If possible, ask participants to bring their own spiritually symbolic items and explain those items to the group as an introductory process for this exercise.

■ After the session, write down and photocopy the lighted candle responses along with a picture or drawing of a candle, and distribute it to participants as a tangible reminder of their experience.

SYMBOLS AND RITUALS

Part I

What are some of your significant spiritual symbols and rituals (for example, a solitary walk in nature, marriage ceremony, funeral, communion service, crucifix, Star of David, ring)?

What do they signify and what messages do they give you (for example, peace, inspiration, wonder, love, commitment, grief, celebration, humility, devotion)?

My symbols/rituals   Their meaning

_____   _____

_____   _____

_____   _____

_____   _____

_____   _____

How have these symbols and rituals been helpful to you in your life?

_____

_____

_____

What additional symbols or rituals might you find helpful to you in the future? _____

_____

_____

_____

Part II

Record a summary of your thoughts, observations, and insights:

_____

_____

_____

Supplementary Resources

SUPPLEMENTARY RESOURCES

DEALING WITH DIFFICULT ISSUES   (p 133)

ADAPTING THE GROUP FOR THE COGNITIVELY IMPAIRED   (p 143)

GROUP OBSERVATION QUESTIONS   (p 144)

SELECTED BIBLIOGRAPHY   (p 146)

DEALING WITH DIFFICULT ISSUES

During the development of the spiritual awareness groups, we recognized 20 sensitive issues that arise from time to time. We hesitate to call them problems, but they can become so if not dealt with effectively during the group session.

We brainstormed ideas with peers, searched the literature, and learned by trial and error. Our ideas and suggestions are designed to foster comfort and ease tension as effectively as possible when difficult issues arise. The list is, of course, still in the process of development as we continue to learn ourselves. We will appreciate receiving word of additional suggestions that you find effective as you struggle with these same leadership challenges.

We can't say what will work in your setting, but here's a list of ideas we have found useful.

1. Anger in the group setting

- Be alert to anger, either expressed directly or indirectly. Do not personalize participants' expression of anger.
- Is the reason for the anger appropriate for you to process in the group context? If not, acknowledge the anger and focus on the meaning of the experience.
- Ask angry people if they can recall a time they did not feel this way? What contributed to the change? What has been helpful in previous times of anger?
- Offer limited time to vent; provide equal time for positive statements.
- If the behavior is too disruptive, ask the group member to leave the group. The danger is that the angry person may monopolize and attempt to control the group.
- Remember that anger is a part of the grieving process and may lead to healing. It is also a way to mobilize energy.
- Acknowledging, validating, and supporting the expression of anger by facilitating appropriate ventilation can be therapeutic.
- Ask if others have had the same or a similar experience? What has been helpful?
- Focus on the positive aspects of the experience.
- Use exercises that focus on addressing anger issues, for example, the **Guilt and Forgiveness** and **God's Presence** exercises.

- Consider whether the person is expressing anxiety rather than anger. Encourage identification and acknowledgment of feelings. Allow time to process these feelings.

2. Anger at God or religion

- Acknowledge and validate the feelings of the member.
- Leaders need to recognize their own feelings about anger at God and to recognize the possibility of countertransference.
- Avoid defensiveness when a group member criticizes a certain religion or set of beliefs—recognize and accept your feelings as a leader.
- Acknowledge that the member's feelings are a real and not uncommon experience.
- Encourage members to respond to each other.
- Encourage discussion of how others have coped with their experiences.
- Use exercises that have a focus on addressing anger issues. For example, the **Guilt and Forgiveness** or **God's Presence** exercises.
- Affirm the positive aspects of the experience.
- Reflect on the fact that, in the presence of empathetic and objective listeners, healing can occur from the expression of anger and pain.

3. Proselytizing behaviors (attempts to convert other participants)

- During the introduction to the group session, explain that the purpose is not to try to convert anyone, but to share beliefs and accumulated wisdom, with respect for the expression of diverse views.
- When a person proselytizes or preaches during the session, draw the person's attention to the experiences in his or her life that have contributed to the strength of his or her belief.
- Acknowledge the member's strength and commitment without focusing on the specific belief, that is, explore how the person nurtures his or her beliefs.
- Do not make any statements that indicate that you think the belief is right or wrong.
- Encourage and support the appropriate expression of the participant's unique life experiences that contribute to the formation of beliefs. A participant may want to tell the group how or why his or her belief is the only way to believe. While neither agreeing or disagreeing with the belief, the leader can focus on the experiences in life that led the person to believe with that much conviction. The leader may also ask how this belief has been supported and nurtured by the participant.

©1995 Whole Person Press 210 W Michigan Duluth MN 55802   (800) 247-6789

- Acknowledge, affirm, and validate appropriate sharing of experiences and emphasize commonalities, but affirm the right of people to formulate their own beliefs.

- In some cases, intervention may be needed in which the leader again clearly states that the purpose of the group is not to convince and convict others but to share experiences. The leader then states the need to move on, allowing others to participate.

- If this behavior is anticipated, speak to the group member about your concerns prior to the group. Do this in a way that acknowledges and helps to maintain the individual's sense of dignity and integrity.

- If this behavior is still anticipated, select a less religiously oriented theme.

- Maintain respect for appropriate expression of each person's belief system. Remember that the focus of the group is shared wisdom, finding meaning by identifying experiences, and discovering questions, concerns and areas of struggle.

4. Monopolizing, hyperverbal, or disruptive behaviors

- Address boundaries and limits during the introduction to the session.
- Provide structure.
- Set limits on all disruptive or monopolizing behaviors.
- Allow time for each member to participate.
- Assure talkative members that they will have another opportunity to participate.
- Ask overly talkative members to be group assistants (to read poetry, assist with refreshments, etc.).
- Try to redirect.
- Give a warning, clearly identifying the behavior in a diplomatic manner. If the behavior remains unchanged, ask the member to leave, informing the person that you would like to talk with him or her after the group. If the group is part of an inpatient program, inform the person's primary caretaker of the incident. Discuss this disruption briefly with the group and continue to move on. Follow up with the disruptive person after the session.

5. Moving from a superficial to a more personal level

- Use questions that direct members to a feeling level: How do you feel about what you just said? It must be very difficult for you to say that.
- Mention that some things may be difficult to talk about, and that is okay. We can talk about why it may be difficult.

- Avoid affirmations that place a right or wrong value on the person's comment. Instead, affirm the person for his or her contribution. Affirm each group member for the contributions made.
- Ask how the participants have experienced or supported their beliefs in life.
- Use clarification questions. For example: I got confused. Did anyone else? Can you explain further?
- When applicable, say: I feel concerned about _____. Does anyone else feel that way? Can you explain your concern?
- Encourage participants to respond to each other's contributions.
- When meeting with older people, do not assume that certain topics are too painful or sensitive for discussion.
- Recognize and avoid you own bias when discussing such things, for example, sex, abuse, or death.
- Utilize third person comments and questions. For example: Some people who experience suffering feel that God is unfair to them. What do you think regarding God in this matter? Some people who work hard and long hours throughout their lives find it very boring, or feel unfulfilled, after the children are raised or retirement occurs. How have you experienced this time of your life?
- Avoid pat responses. Statements such as "Love conquers all," or "No pain, no gain," discount and invalidate the person's beliefs and feelings.
- Advice from a leader may suggest that easy answers are available, therefore minimizing the member's concerns and feelings.
- Periodically summarize what has been said. Emphasize the threads of common experiences and feelings.

6. Prayer in the group

- At the end of the session, ask for suggestions from members as to how they would like to close the group.
- If prayer is suggested, ask if all the members concur with this suggestion.
- If objections are offered, counter by closing with a brief time of silence. A second alternative is to ask each member to complete the following sentence: "I am thankful for _____ (hope, life, etc.)," or "I wish the group _____ (peace, health, etc.)."
- If it is indicated and if the leaders are familiar with the participants, ask if someone would like to lead the group in a short prayer.
- Remember that the goal is to maintain universality.

7. Suicide or discussion of suicide

- If suicide is discussed, focus on how other choices can be made: What are some other options? What would help you make other choices?

- Ask how the thought of suicide affects or relates to spiritual beliefs?

- Ask the group who experiences the impact of suicide—what they believe about the impact that suicide has on the living?

- Consider options for support and strength in times of extreme hopelessness?

8. Comments about Satan: dealing with issues of evil

- Assess potential members for delusional symptoms, religious preoccupation, or hallucinations that would contraindicate attending a spiritually oriented group.

- If comments are not congruent with the session theme, redirect to the central topic and focus.

- Reflect to the group that Satan is viewed as a symbol of evil, regardless of people's belief or disbelief.

- Ask how other members have dealt with a sense of evil (if applicable to the theme).

- State, _____ has experienced evil in this way. How have other members experienced it?

- Avoid any focus on right or wrong, or trueness or falseness of the person's belief. It is especially important for leaders to understand that they should not try to prove or disprove the existence of an objective entity called Satan.

- Ask the individual to give concrete examples of experiences that demonstrate concerns about evil.

- Determine how the belief or concern contributes to or affects the person's life. Ask if the belief had a positive or negative effect in the person's life?

- If the person's sense of evil is intense, ask if the individual has ever spoken to a pastor, rabbi, or other spiritual advisor, about these beliefs.

- Recommend that the person speak to a spiritual advisor. Offer to talk about this privately.

- Some people think of spirituality in terms of spiritual warfare. They see themselves as players in the great cosmic battle between good and evil, between God and Satan. If a person talks about spirituality in these terms, ask the individual about methods of focusing on the good. Ask how this person's belief in God helps in the battle with Satan.

9. Countertransference, transference, myths, and bias

- As the leader, keep in mind that as we address issues of spirituality, we come face to face with our own issues about spirituality.

- Do not assume that certain subjects such as sex, intimacy, abuse, and death may be too painful for people to discuss. Try to become aware of your own bias. Don't project your anxiety on the group.

- Recognize, acknowledge, and discuss your fears, concerns, potential bias, and beliefs privately with a colleague, supervisor, or selected spiritual adviser.

- Role playing scenarios of challenging situations is recommended.

- Maintain ongoing self awareness, objectivity, and openness.

- Process thoughts, concerns, and feelings with coleaders in pre- and post-group discussions.

- Participants may project their own issues on other group members or the group leader. Be aware of this potential when comments directed to others seem inappropriate.

- If leaders are comfortable during discussion, group members will also be comfortable.

10. Religious doubt

- Affirm the value of openly expressing feelings and beliefs, including doubt.

- Remember that doubt can be an indicator of belief formation.

- Encourage participants to discuss their concerns with a spiritual friend or pastor.

- Remember that it is not the role of the leader to resolve doubt but rather to create an environment that permits the expression of doubt and provides for the exploration of feelings.

- Does the person feel guilty about doubt? What experience might be precipitating this doubt?

- Specific issues of theology and doctrine should be referred to an individual's personal spiritual advisor.

11. The meaning in suffering

- When people are hurting, they often ask questions that are unanswerable.

- Be aware of the phases of normal grieving. Listen to the person expressing grief. Validate the person's feelings and recognize the person's pain.

- Recognize that in suffering, people are searching for the meaning of the pain.

- Be honest in acknowledging that you do not know the answers. Be present through the search. Be an empathetic and objective listener. Recognize and reflect to the group that there is a healing value in supporting the ventilation of pain and the appropriate expression of an individual's experience. It is not the leader's or listener's responsibility to make it better, but to provide support.

- Ask participants to describe a time of pain or suffering and identify what they learned from the experience and whether it helped them at other times in their life? Ask them to describe a time they were able to help, support, or comfort someone else because they had experienced suffering.

- Support moving the discussion from "Why me?" questions to identifying alternatives, methods of support, and growth from the experience.

12. Extreme negativity

- In cases of disruptive hopelessness, ask the individual what, specifically, he or she is experiencing.

- Make a process statement (an observation).

- Ask the person to share his or her feelings.

- Request input from other members of the group.

- Acknowledge that we always have choices and identify some more positive options.

13. Sexuality and intimacy

- A variety of terms have been used to guide the discussion in these areas: intimacy, sexuality, romance, passion, love, etc.

- Remember that this is a topic of importance for all ages.

- Be aware of your own potential discomfort when discussing this topic.

14. Disclosure of religious preference

- When people challenge the religious denomination of others, they will need to be redirected.

- You may need to state that the purpose of the group is to share experiences and beliefs without a focus on specific religious preference.

- Reflect to the group that, although there may be diversity of ideology or theology, there are common bonds of feelings and experience.

- Be aware of policies and practices regarding personal self-disclosure and professional boundaries.

15. When reminiscing is too painful

- Although it happens infrequently, there are times when people find reminiscing to be too painful to experience. This may be due to extreme tragedy or a history of abuse.

- If someone becomes upset, offer support and do not probe further *at that time*. Other members of the group may also want to offer support. It may then be appropriate to focus the individual or group on the present or future.

- You may choose to say: I can see that these memories are very painful for you. I'd like to move on to another subject, but I would like to talk to you right after this session.

- The idea is not to change the subject to avoid the pain but to help the individual deal with his or her feelings in a private, safer way.

- Immediately after the group session, help the individual process the painful feelings evoked by the memories. There are many themes that can be adapted to emphasize strength and wisdom and to focus on present or future orientation. This focus is recommended when reminiscing is too painful.

16. Questions of religion and spirituality

- Recognize that people often are not able to make a clear distinction between the two.

- Define spirituality as our personal relationship to the transcendent (God, or our interpretation of God) and religion as the form in which that relationship is expressed.

- Help members to recognize that religion, with its particular system of beliefs, rules of conduct, and rituals, serves as a vehicle for the expression of spirituality. Spirituality is the way we orient ourselves to the divine and provides a perspective to foster purpose, meaning, and direction to life.

- Identify simple ways of meeting spiritual needs. For example, people might enjoy a view, take a nature walk, read a verse, poem or greeting card, exercise, meditate, enjoy humor. They might find or become empathetic listeners.

17. Assessing religious preoccupation

- Religious preoccupation needs to be assessed cautiously and objectively to determine whether or not there is an underlying thought disorder.

- If there is an indication of a thought disorder, the individual should not be included in the group until stabilized.

©1995 Whole Person Press 210 W Michigan Duluth MN 55802   (800) 247-6789

18. The language of spirituality

- Initially, because of personal discomfort with some of the terminology and a sincere desire to remain unbiased, there is a hesitancy on the part of new leaders to use the language of spirituality when dealing with people with diverse ideas.

- Individuals must be allowed to refer to God and to their values, beliefs, and experiences in the terms that they are comfortable with. This can be done without compromise to the leader's personal or professional integrity. For example, if a members says, Jesus is Lord, the leader might respond by saying: It sounds like you have a strong belief. What brought you to knowing Jesus as your Lord?

19. Awesome moments

- In our fast-paced work environments, we sometimes are left with brief moments of contact with those in our care. All too often the same can happen in our personal lives.

- Through heart and soul communication we can turn those moments into times of deep and significant discovery—awesome moments. These moments await us; they may come suddenly and unexpectedly, or they may be deliberately cultivated.

- The techniques and principles of communication provided in this manual and used in the group setting can be applied to brief or to extended interactions in both our personal and professional lives. If we are willing to overcome barriers, we can open the door to touching moments of spiritual contact. This can result in life giving insights for both the listener and receiver. The following steps will open the door:

    Be open to the experience.

    Use active listening and sensitive hearing.

    Encourage the sharing of genuine feelings.

    Relinquish preset opinions.

    Be willing to learn and grow.

20. Loss and termination

- If, for some reason, a group participant is unable to attend a session, it is important to acknowledge this absence.

- If a participant is no longer able to attend the group, provide time for the group members to express their thoughts and feelings about this loss. The departing member may want to share his or her goals for the future

©1995 Whole Person Press 210 W Michigan Duluth MN 55802   (800) 247-6789

with the group. The leader and all members can be given the opportunity to express appreciation for having had the opportunity to be with each other.

- If a member of the group dies, it is particularly important to acknowledge the loss and to give people time to grieve.

©1995 Whole Person Press 210 W Michigan Duluth MN 55802   (800) 247-6789

ADAPTING THE GROUP
FOR THE COGNITIVELY IMPAIRED

Exercises, techniques, and guidelines for the group process can be adapted for cognitively impaired participants.

For these members, advanced preparation for the group should include obtaining information from a family member, friend, or an informed caregiver. This enables the leader to gain perspective on the spiritual affiliation and the spiritual needs of the participant.

A symbol for the session, such as a lighted candle, floral bouquet, or a scenic picture of nature, will provide a pleasant and comfortable focal point. Group members can be encouraged to contribute a centerpiece and then offered appreciation for sharing this with the group.

Props and resources are very effective with people who are cognitively impaired. Try to appeal to all the senses with memorabilia, pictures, scents, food, and music. Items such as these evoke recollection and encourages discussion, and are a way to bring members into contact with reality.

Memory is stimulated by encouraging members to recall and recite verses of poetry and to sing familiar inspirational music.

Use the chalkboard to focus attention and reinforce discussion. Consider the participants attention span. Twenty to thirty minutes may be a sufficiently long session.

Be aware of sensory impairment and the need to repeat questions. Avoid pushing or probing for responses by accepting the expressions that each member can contribute. Be flexible and tolerant about interruptions.

The exercises **Group Poetry**, **Word Flower**, **Word Expansion**, **Favorite Sayings**, **Faith**, **Senses**, and **Wisdom** are suggested for use with the cognitively impaired.

©1995 Whole Person Press 210 W Michigan Duluth MN 55802   (800) 247-6789

GROUP OBSERVATION QUESTIONS

The topics below can be used to help group leaders improve their skills. They will be particularly useful if a group has coleaders, but even when there is only one leader, evaluation is essential.

1. Pre-group preparation

- Was advance notice given to group members? Methods:
- Was pre-group planning done? Describe:
- Was a pre-group discussion with coleader conducted?
- Were resources gathered prior to group? What?
- Was the group room prepared prior to group? How?
- Did the group start on time? If not, why?

2. Group format

- Were the following items addressed in the introduction?

      Group purpose

      Meeting place

      Time

      Confidentiality

- Was a warm-up question used? Why or why not?
- Identify the theme discussed.
- Were any props used? What items?
- What closing method was used?

3. Group process

- How did the leader create or establish an open, honest, safe, and nonthreatening environment?
- How was group ownership encouraged and demonstrated?
- Were there self-disclosure issues? Describe them.
- What methods were used to evoke discussion?
- What methods were used to move discussion from a superficial level to a more personal level?
- What techniques were used to develop and expand discussion?

- How were contributions of participants validated?
- Was there an emphasis on using past strengths and wisdom gained from past strengths? Was the use of these strengths in the present and future explored?
- How was the discussion summarized prior to closing?
- Describe your views of the differences you observed in the older and younger population in the areas of participation, values, and belief formation, and the expression of beliefs and experiences.
- If it was necessary to set limits on a participant's behavior, explain why and how this was done.
- Describe the leadership style that was used.

4. Post group procedures

- If the group was co-led, was the session discussed and evaluated by both leaders?
- Was a written summary of the session made?
- Were resources returned to their proper locations?
- What did you learn from the session?
- How could you improve your skills? Identify several goals.

©1995 Whole Person Press 210 W Michigan Duluth MN 55802   (800) 247-6789

SELECTED BIBLIOGRAPHY

Anderson, R. G., and J. L. Young. 1988. The religious component of acute hospital treatment. *Hospital and Community Psychiatry, 39*(5), 528–32.

Baker, N. 1985. Reminiscing in group therapy for self-worth. *Journal of Gerontological Nursing, 1*(7), 21–24.

Burnside, I. (Ed.). 1986. *Working with the elderly: Group process and techniques* (2nd ed.). Boston: Jones and Bartlett Publishers, Inc.

_____. 1988. *Nursing and the aged: A self care approach* (3rd ed.). New York: McGraw Hill

Britnell, J., and K. Mitchell. 1981. Inpatient group psychotherapy for the elderly. *Psychiatric Nursing, 19*(5), 19–24.

Butler, R. N., and M. T. Lewis. 1974. Life review therapy. *Geriatrics, 9*(11), 165–173.

Butler, R. N., M. T. Lewis, and T. Sunderland. 1991. *Aging and mental health: Positive psychosocial and biomedical approaches.* New York: Macmillan Publishing Company.

Carson, V. 1980. Meeting the spiritual needs of hospitalized psychiatric patients. *Perspectives in Psychiatric Care, 18*(1), 17–20.

Chaffee, P., J. Favor, W. Moremen, F. Oliver, and F. Wuellner. 1989. *Spirit awakening: A book of practices.* San Francisco: Spiritual Priority Publishing Group.

Cox, H., and A. Hammonds. 1988. Religiosity, aging and life satisfaction. *Journal of Religion and Aging, 5*(1/2), 1–21.

deMello, Anthony. 1985. *Wellsprings: A Book of Spiritual Exercises.* New York: Doubleday and Company, Inc.

Fabry, J. 1968. *The pursuit of meaning.* Boston: Beacon Press.

Farran, C., G. Fitchett, J. Quiring-Emblen, and J. Burck. 1989. Development of a model for spiritual assessment and intervention. *Journal of Religion and Health, 28*(3), 185–194.

Feil, N. 1989. *Validation: The Feil method.* Cleveland, OH: Edward Feil Productions.

Fischer, K. 1985. *Winter grace: Spirituality for the later years.* New York: Paulist Press.

_____. 1989. *Wisdom and wonder in later years.* [Public Forum on Cassette]. Spokane, Washington: Sacred Heart Medical Center.

_____. 1989. *Wonder and wisdom in later years: Spirituality, morality and aging.* [Workshop on Cassette]. Spokane, Washington: Sacred Heart Medical Center.

Haight, B. 1989. Life review: A method for pastoral counseling: Part I. *Journal of Religion and Aging, 5*(3), 17–29.

_____. 1991. Reminiscing: The state of the art as a basis for practice. *International Journal of Aging and Human Development, 33*(1), 1–32.

Haight, B. and I. Burnside. 1992. Reminiscing and life review: Conducting the process. *Journal of Gerontological Nursing, 18*(2), 39–42.

Henderson, K. J. 1989. Dying, God and anger: Comforting through spiritual care. *Journal of Psychosocial Nursing, 27*(5), 17–21, 31–32.

Ivy, S. 1985. *The structural developmental theories of James Fowler and Robert Kegan as resources for pastoral assessment.* Ann Arbor: University Microfilms International.

Kaminsky, M. 1984. *The uses of reminiscence: New ways of working with older adults.* New York: The Haworth Press, Inc.

Katz, R. and B. Genevay. 1987. Older people, dying and countertransference. *Generations, 12*(2), 28–32.

Kivnick, H. 1993. Everyday mental health: A guide to assessing life strengths. *Generations, 17*(1), 13–20.

Koenig, H., L. George, and I. Siegler. 1988. The use of religion and other emotion-regulating coping strategies among older adults. *The Gerontologist, 28*(3), 303–310.

Koch, K. 1977. *I never told anybody: Teaching poetry writing in nursing homes.* New York: Random House.

Krohn, B. 1989. Spiritual care: The forgotten need. *NSNA/Imprint, 36*(1), 95–6.

Nadzo, S. C. 1980. *There is a way.* New York: Coleman Publishers Inc.

Nelson, P. B. 1990. Intrinsic/extrinsic religious orientation of the elderly: Relationship to depression and self-esteem. *Journal of Gerontological Nursing, 16*(2), 29–37.

Oleson, M. 1989. News, notes and tips: Legacies, reminiscence and ego-integrity: (Case Study). *Nurse Educator, 14*(6), 26, 31, 35, 39.

Piles, C. 1990. Providing spiritual care. *Nurse Educator, 15*(1), 36–41.

Poulton, J. L., and D. S. Strassberg. 1986. The therapeutic use of reminiscence. *International Journal of Group Psychotherapy, 36*(3), 381–398.

Richards, M. 1990. Meeting the spiritual needs of the cognitively impaired. *Generations, 4*(4), 63–4.

Rico, G. L. 1983. *Writing the natural way*. Los Angeles: J. P. Tarcher, Inc.

Sherman, E. 1993. Mental health and successful adaptation in later life. *Generations, 17*(1), 43–6.

Sims, C. 1987. Spiritual care as a part of holistic nursing. *NSNA/Imprint, 24*(4), 63–5.

Sukosky, G. G. 1989. Disengagement and life review: The possible relevance of integrating theological perspectives. *Journal of Religion and Aging, 5*(4), 1–14.

Taft, L. 1989. Remembering and sharing through poetry writing. *Nurse Educator, 14*(1), 37–38.

Widerquist, J. 1991. Another view on spiritual care [Guest Editorial]. *Nurse Educator, 16*(2), 5–6.

©1995 Whole Person Press 210 W Michigan Duluth MN 55802　　　(800) 247-6789

Whole Person Associates Resources

All printed, audio, and video resources developed by Whole Person Associates are designed to address the whole person—physical, emotional, mental, spiritual, and social. On the next pages, trainers will find a wide array of resources that offer ready-to-use ideas and concepts they can add to their programs.

RELAXATION RESOURCES

Many trainers and workshop leaders have discovered the benefits of relaxation and visualization in healing the body, mind, and spirit.

30 SCRIPTS FOR RELAXATION, IMAGERY, AND INNER HEALING
Julie Lusk

The relaxation scripts, creative visualizations and guided meditations in these volumes were created by experts in the field of guided imagery. Julie Lusk collected their best and most effective scripts to help novices get started and experienced leaders expand their repertoire. Both volumes include information on how to use the scripts, suggestions for tailoring them to specific needs and audiences, and information on how to successfully incorporate guided imagery into existing programs.

❏ **30 Scripts**
   Volume 1 & 2 / $19.95 each

GUIDED IMAGERY FOR GROUPS
Andrew Schwartz

Ideal for courses, workshops, team building, and personal stress management, this comprehensive resource includes scripts for 50 thematic visualizations that promote calming, centering, creativity, congruence, clarity, coping, and connectedness. Detailed instructions for using relaxation techniques and guided images in group settings allow educators at all levels, in any setting, to help people tap into the healing and creative powers of imagery.

❏ **Guided Imagery for Groups / $24.95**

INQUIRE WITHIN
Andrew Schwartz

Use visualization to help people make positive changes in their lives. The 24 visualization experiences in **Inquire Within** will help participants enhance their creativity, heal inner pain, learn to relax, and deal with conflict. Each visualization includes questions at the end of the process that encourage deeper reflection and a better understanding of the exercise and the response it evokes.

❏ **Inquire Within / $19.95**

To order, call toll free   (800) 247-6789

STRUCTURED EXERCISES IN STRESS MANAGEMENT

Nancy Loving Tubesing, EdD, and Donald A. Tubesing, PhD, Editors

Each book in this four-volume series contains 36 ready-to-use teaching modules that involve the participant—as a whole person—in learning how to manage stress more effectively.

Each volume brims with practical ideas that mix and match allowing trainers to develop new programs for varied settings, audiences, and time frames. Each volume contains **Icebreakers, Stress Assessments, Management Strategies, Skill Builders, Action Planners, Closing Processes,** and **Group Energizers**.

❑ **Stress 8 1/2" x 11" Loose-Leaf Edition—Volume 1-4 / $54.95 each**
❑ **Stress 6" x 9" Softcover Edition—Volume 1-4 / $29.95 each**

STRUCTURED EXERCISES IN WELLNESS PROMOTION

Nancy Loving Tubesing, EdD, and Donald A. Tubesing, PhD, Editors

Each of the four volumes in this innovative series includes 36 experiential learning activities that focus on whole person health—body, mind, spirit, emotions, relationships, and life-style.

Icebreakers, Wellness Explorations, Self-Care Strategies, Action Planners, Closings, and **Group Energizers** are all ready-to-go—including reproducible worksheets, scripts, and chalktalk outlines—for the busy professional who wants to develop unique wellness programs without spending hours in preparation.

❑ **Wellness 8 1/2" x 11" Loose-Leaf Edition—Volume 1-4 / $54.95 each**
❑ **Wellness 6" x 9" Softcover Edition—Volume 1-4 / $29.95 each**

WORKSHEET MASTERS

Complete packages of (8 1/2" x 11") photocopy masters are available for all **Structured Exercises in Stress Management** and **Structured Exercises in Wellness Promotion**. Use the masters to conveniently duplicate handouts for each participant.

❑ **Worksheet Masters / $9.95 per volume**

To order, call toll free   (800) 247-6789

RELAXATION AUDIOTAPES

Perhaps you're an old hand at relaxation, looking for new ideas. Or maybe you're a beginner, just testing the waters. Whatever your relaxation needs, Whole Person audiotapes provide a whole family of options for reducing physical and mental stress.

Techniques range from simple breathing and stretching exercises to classic autogenic and progressive relaxation sequences, guided meditations, and whimsical daydreams. All are carefully crafted to promote whole person relaxation—body, mind, and spirit.

If you're looking for an extended relaxation experience (20 minutes or more), try a tape from the Sensational Relaxation, Guided Imagery, or Wilderness Daydreams groups. For quick R&R breaks (5–10 minutes), try one from the Stress Breaks, Daydreams or Mini-Meditations collections. All of our tapes feature male and female narrators.

Audiotapes are available for $11.95 each.
Call for generous quantity discounts.

SENSATIONAL RELAXATION—$11.95 each
When stress piles up, it becomes a heavy load both physically and emotionally. These full-length relaxation experiences will teach you techniques that can be used whenever you feel that stress is getting out of control. Choose one you like and repeat it daily until it becomes second nature, then recall that technique whenever you need it or try a new one every day.

- ❏ **Countdown to Relaxation /** Countdown 19:00, Staircase 19:00
- ❏ **Daybreak / Sundown /** Daybreak 22:00, Sundown 22:00
- ❏ **Take a Deep Breath /** Breathing for Relaxation 17:00, Magic Ball 17:00
- ❏ **Relax . . . Let Go . . . Relax /** Revitalization 27:00, Relaxation 28:00
- ❏ **StressRelease /** Quick Tension Relievers 22:00, Progressive Relaxation 20:00
- ❏ **Warm and Heavy /** Warm 24:00, Heavy 23:00

STRESS BREAKS—$11.95 each
Do you need a short energy booster or a quick stress reliever? If you don't know what type of relaxation you like, or if you are new to guided relaxation techniques, try one of our Stress Breaks for a quick refocusing or change of pace any time of the day.

- ❏ **BreakTime /** Solar Power 8:00, Belly Breathing 9:00, Fortune Cookie 9:00, Mother Earth 11:00, Big Yawn 5:00, Affirmation 11:00
- ❏ **Natural Tranquilizers /** Clear the Deck 10:00, Body Scan 10:00, 99 Countdown 10:00, Calm Down 9:00, Soothing Colors 11:00, Breathe Ten 9:00

To order, call toll free (800) 247-6789

DAYDREAMS—$11.95 each
Escape from the stress around you with guided tours to beautiful places. The quick escapes in our Daydreams tapes will lead your imagination away from your everyday cares so you can resume your tasks relaxed and comforted.

- ❏ **Daydreams 1: Getaways /** Cabin Retreat 11:00, Night Sky 10:00, Hot Spring 7:00, Mountain View 8:00, Superior Sail 8:00
- ❏ **Daydreams 2: Peaceful Places /** Ocean Tides 11:00, City Park 10:00, Hammock 8:00, Meadow 11:00
- ❏ **Daydreams 3: Relaxing Retreats /** Melting Candle 5:00, Tropical Paradise 10:00, Sanctuary 7:00, Floating Clouds 5:00, Seasons 9:00, Beach Tides 9:00

GUIDED MEDITATION—$11.95 each
Take a step beyond relaxation. The imagery in our full-length meditations will help you discover your strengths, find healing, make positive life changes, and recognize your inner wisdom.

- ❏ **Inner Healing /** Inner Healing 20:00, Peace with Pain 20:00
- ❏ **Personal Empowering /** My Gifts 22:00, Hidden Strengths 21:00
- ❏ **Healthy Balancing /** Inner Harmony 20:00, Regaining Equilibrium 20:00
- ❏ **Spiritual Centering /** Spiritual Centering 20:00 (male and female narration)

WILDERNESS DAYDREAMS—$11.95 each
Discover the healing power of nature with the four tapes in our Wilderness Daydreams series. The eight special journeys will transport you from your harried, stressful surroundings to the peaceful serenity of words and water.

- ❏ **Canoe / Rain /** Canoe 19:00, Rain 22:00
- ❏ **Island / Spring /** Island 19:00, Spring 19:00
- ❏ **Campfire / Stream /** Campfire 17:00, Stream 19:00
- ❏ **Sailboat / Pond /** Sailboat 25:00, Pond 25:00

MINI-MEDITATIONS—$11.95 each
These brief guided visualizations begin by focusing your breathing and uncluttering your mind, so that you can concentrate on a sequence of sensory images that promote relaxation, centering, healing, growth, and spiritual awareness.

- ❏ **Healing Visions /** Rocking Chair 5:00, Pine Forest 8:00, Long Lost Confidant 10:00, Caterpillar to Butterfly 7:00, Superpowers 9:00, Tornado 8:00
- ❏ **Refreshing Journeys /** 1 to 10 10:00, Thoughts Library 11:00, Visualizing Change 6:00, Magic Carpet 9:00, Pond of Love 9:00, Cruise 9:00

MUSIC ONLY—$11.95 each
No relaxation program would be complete without relaxing melodies that can be played as background to a prepared script or that can be enjoyed as you practice a technique you have already learned. Steven Eckels composed his melodies specifically for relaxation. These "musical prayers for healing" will calm your body, mind, and spirit.

- ❏ **Tranquility /** Awakening 20:00, Repose 20:00
- ❏ **Harmony /** Waves of Light 30:00, Rising Mist 10:00, Frankincense 10:00, Angelica 10:00
- ❏ **Serenity /** Radiance 20:00, Quiessence 10:00, Evanesence 10:00

To order, call toll free   (800) 247-6789

GROUP PROCESS RESOURCES

All of the exercises in these group process resources encourage interaction between the leader and participants, as well as among the participants. Each exercise includes everything needed to present a meaningful program.

WORKING WITH WOMEN'S GROUPS
Volumes 1 & 2

Louise Yolton Eberhardt

The two volumes of **Working with Women's Groups** have been completely revised and updated. **Volume 1** explores consciousness raising, self-discovery, and assertiveness training. **Volume 2** looks at sexuality issues, women of color, and leadership skills training.

❑ **Working with Women's Groups**
Volumes 1 & 2 / $24.95 per volume

WORKING WITH MEN'S GROUPS

Roger Karsk and Bill Thomas

Working with Men's Groups has been updated to reflect the reality of men's lives in the 1990s. Each exercise follows a structured pattern to help trainers develop either onetime workshops or ongoing groups that explore men's issues in four key areas: self-discovery, consciousness raising, intimacy, and parenting.

❑ **Working with Men's Groups / $24.95**

WORKSHEET MASTERS

Complete packages of (8 1/2" x 11") photocopy masters are available for **Working with Women's Groups** and **Working with Men's Groups**. Use the masters to conveniently duplicate handouts for each participant.

❑ **Worksheet Masters / $9.95 per volume**

WORKSHOPS-IN-A-BOOK

Workshops-in-a-book are developed to be used as a classroom text, discussion guide, and participant workbook; a professional resource for both novice and experienced trainers; a personal journey for individuals; all in an easy-to-understand, user-friendly format.

KICKING YOUR STRESS HABITS:
A Do-it-yourself Guide for Coping with Stress
Donald A. Tubesing, PhD

Over a quarter of a million people have found ways to deal with their everyday stress by using **Kicking Your Stress Habits**. This workshop-in-a-book actively involves the reader in assessing stressful patterns and developing more effective coping strategies with helpful "Stop and Reflect" sections in each chapter.

The 10-step planning process and 20 skills for managing stress make **Kicking Your Stress Habits** an ideal text for stress management classes in many different settings, from hospitals to universities.

❑ **Kicking Your Stress Habits / $14.95**

SEEKING YOUR HEALTHY BALANCE:
A Do-it-yourself Guide to Whole Person Well-being
Donald A. Tubesing, PhD and Nancy Loving Tubesing, EdD

Where can people find the time and energy to "do it all" without sacrificing health and well-being? **Seeking Your Healthy Balance** helps readers discover how to develop a more balanced life-style by learning effective ways to juggle work, self, and others; by clarifying self-care options; and by discovering and setting their own personal priorities.

Seeking Your Healthy Balance asks the questions that help readers find their own answers.

❑ **Seeking Your Healthy Balance / $14.95**

To order, call toll free   (800) 247-6789

VIDEO RESOURCES

These video-based workshops use the power of professionally produced videotapes as a starting point. Then they build on the experience with printed guides chock-full of suggestions, group processes, and personal growth exercises that build sessions participants will remember!

MAKING HEALTHY CHOICES

Making Healthy Choices, a complete six-session, video-based course on healthy living, encourages people to begin making the choices, large and small, that promote wellness in all areas of their lives. Save $95.00 by purchasing the complete set or select individual sessions.

- ❏ **MAKING HEALTHY CHOICES SET / $475.00**
- ❏ **Healthy Lifestyle / $95.00**
- ❏ **Healthy Eating / $95.00**
- ❏ **Healthy Exercise / $95.00**
- ❏ **Healthy Stress / $95.00**
- ❏ **Healthy Relationships / $95.00**
- ❏ **Healthy Change / $95.00**

MANAGING JOB STRESS

Managing Job Stress, a comprehensive six-session stress management course, takes aim at a universal problem: work-related stress. Each session emphasizes positive responses to the challenges of on-the-job stress. Save $95.00 by purchasing the entire set or select individual sessions.

- ❏ **MANAGING JOB STRESS SET / $475.00**
- ❏ **Handling Workplace Pressure / $95.00**
- ❏ **Clarifying Roles and Expectations / $95.00**
- ❏ **Controlling the Workload / $95.00**
- ❏ **Managing People Pressures / $95.00**
- ❏ **Surviving the Changing Workplace / $95.00**
- ❏ **Balancing Work and Home / $95.00**

MANAGE IT!

Manage It! is an innovative six-part video-based series that helps participants develop management skills for handling stress. Participants learn new coping skills and practice a relaxation technique for immediate on-the-spot stress relief. Save $95.00 by purchasing the entire set or select individual sessions.

- ❏ **MANAGE IT! SET / $475.00**
- ❏ **Stress Traps / $95.00**
- ❏ **Stress Overload / $95.00**
- ❏ **Interpersonal Conflict / $95.00**
- ❏ **Addictive Patterns / $95.00**
- ❏ **Job Stress / $95.00**
- ❏ **Survival Skills / $95.00**

To order, call toll free   (800) 247-6789

PLAYFUL ACTIVITIES FOR POWERFUL PRESENTATIONS
Bruce Williamson

Spice up presentations with healthy laughter. The 40 creative energizers in *Playful Activities for Powerful Presentations* will enhance learning, stimulate communication, promote teamwork, and reduce resistance to group interaction.

This potent but lighthearted resource will make presentations on any topic more powerful and productive.

❏ **Playful Activities for Powerful Presentations / $19.95**

WORKING WITH GROUPS FROM DYSFUNCTIONAL FAMILIES
Cheryl Hetherington

Even the healthiest family can be dysfunctional at times, making everyone vulnerable to the pain of difficult family relationships.

This collection of 29 proven group activities is designed to heal the pain that results from living in a dysfunctional family. With these exercises leaders can promote healing, build self-esteem, encourage sharing, and help participants acknowledge their feelings.

❏ **Working with Groups from Dysfunctional Families / $24.95**

WORKSHEET MASTERS
A complete package of (8 1/2" x 11") photocopy masters is available for **Working with Groups from Dysfunctional Families**. Use the masters to conveniently duplicate handouts for each participant.
   ❏ **Worksheet Masters / $9.95 per volume**

To order, call toll free   (800) 247-6789

WELLNESS ACTIVITIES FOR YOUTH
Volumes 1 & 2

Sandy Queen

Each volume of **Wellness Activities for Youth** provides 36 complete classroom activities that help leaders teach children and teenagers about wellness with a whole person approach and an emphasis on FUN.

The concepts include:

- values
- stress and coping
- self-esteem
- personal well-being
- social wellness

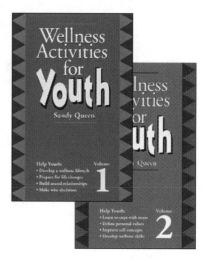

❏ **Wellness Activities for Youth Volume 1 & 2 / $19.95 each**

WORKSHEET MASTERS
Complete packages of (8 1/2" x 11") photocopy masters are available for each volume of **Wellness Activities for Youth**. Use the masters to conveniently duplicate handouts for each participant.

❏ **Worksheet Masters / $9.95 per volume**

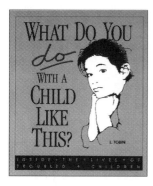

WHAT DO YOU DO WITH A CHILD LIKE THIS?
L. Tobin

What Do You Do With A Child Like This? takes readers on a journey inside the world of troubled children, inviting empathy, then presenting a variety of proven techniques for helping these children to make the behavior changes that will bring them happier lives. This unique book, filled with innovative and practical tools for teachers, psychologists, and parents has been praised by educators for its sensitivity to the pain of troubled kids.

❏ **What Do You Do With A Child Like This? / $14.95**

To order, call toll free   (800) 247-6789

WORKING WITH GROUPS IN THE WORKPLACE

This collection addresses the special needs and concerns of trainers in the workplace. As the work force changes, EAP counselors, education departments, and management are being called on to guide and support their employees who face the challenges of a more diverse workplace.

BRIDGING THE GENDER GAP
Louise Yolton Eberhardt

Bridging the Gender Gap contains a wealth of exercises for the trainer to use with men and women who work as colleagues. These activities will also be useful in gender role awareness groups, diversity training, couples workshops, college classes, and youth seminars.

❏ **Bridging the Gender Gap / $24.95**

CONFRONTING SEXUAL HARASSMENT
Louise Yolton Eberhardt

Confronting Sexual Harassment presents exercises that trainers can safely use with groups to constructively explore the issues of sexual harassment, look at the underlying causes, understand the law, motivate men to become allies, and empower women to speak up.

❏ **Confronting Sexual Harassment / $24.95**

CELEBRATING DIVERSITY
Cheryl Hetherington

Celebrating Diversity helps people confront and question the beliefs, prejudices, and fears that can separate them from others. Carefully written exercises help trainers present these sensitive issues in the workplace as well as in educational settings.

❏ **Celebrating Diversity / $24.95**

WORKSHEET MASTERS
Complete packages of (8 1/2" x 11") photocopy masters are available for all books in the **Working with Groups in the Workplace** series.

❏ **Worksheet Masters / $9.95 per volume**

To order, call toll free   (800) 247-6789

About Whole Person Associates

At Whole Person Associates, we're 100% commit-
ted to providing stress and wellness materials that
involve participants and provide a "whole person"
focus—body, mind, spirit, and relationships.

That's our mission and it's very important to us—
but it doesn't tell the whole story. Behind the products in our catalog is a company full of people—
and *that's* what really makes us who we are.

ABOUT THE OWNERS
Whole Person Associates was created by the vision of two people: Donald A.
Tubesing, PhD, and Nancy Loving Tubesing, EdD. Since way back in 1970, Don
and Nancy have been active in the stress management/wellness promotion
movement—consulting, leading seminars, writing, and publishing. Most of our
early products were the result of their creativity and expertise.

Living proof that you can "stay evergreen," Don and Nancy remain the driving
force behind the company and are still very active in developing new products
that touch people's lives.

ABOUT THE COMPANY
Whole Person Associates was "born" in Duluth, Minnesota, and we remain com-
mitted to our lovely city on the shore of Lake Superior. All of our operations are
here, which makes communication between departments much easier! We've
grown since our beginnings, but at a steady pace—we're interested in sustain-
able growth that allows us to keep our down-to-earth orientation.

We put the same high quality into every product we offer, translating the best of
current research into practical, accessible, easy-to-use materials. In this way
we can create the best possible resources to help our customers teach about
stress management and wellness promotion.

We also strive to treat our customers as we would like to be treated. If we fall
short of our goals in any way, please let us know.

ABOUT OUR EMPLOYEES
Speaking of down-to-earth, that's a requirement for each and every one of our
employees. We're all product consultants, which means that anyone who
answers the phone can probably answer your questions (if they can't, they'll find
someone who can.)

We focus on helping you find the products that fit your needs. And we've found
that the best way to accomplish that is by hiring friendly and resourceful people.

ABOUT OUR ASSOCIATES

Who are the "associates" in Whole Person Associates? They're the trainers, authors, musicians, and others who have developed much of the material you see on these pages. We're always on the lookout for high-quality products that reflect our "whole person" philosophy and fill a need for our customers.

Most of our products were developed by experts who are at the top of their fields, and we're very proud to be associated with them.

ABOUT OUR CUSTOMERS

Finally, we wouldn't have a reason to exist without you, our customers. We've met some of you, and we've talked to many more of you on the phone. We are always aware that without you, there would be no Whole Person Associates.

That's why we'd love to hear from you! Let us know what you think of our products—how you use them in your work, what additional products you'd like to see, and what shortcomings you've noted. Write us or call on our toll-free line. We look forward to hearing from you!